Prenatal Child Support Across the United States

3rd Edition

©2020, 2021 Daniel Gump. All Rights Reserved.

Acknowledgements

I would like to take a moment to thank the amazing free Internet resources provided by sources like the *Hathi Trust Digital Library*[1], *Google*[2], the *Library of Congress*[3], and the numerous state archives, legislative websites, and universities, that make digitized copies of legislation and law reviews available for research. When I wasn't able to find documents online, some great curators of legislative archives were happy to assist, some going way beyond what was necessary. Thank you to Aaron, Dianne, Janice, and Maureen.

I would also like to take a moment to thank the friends who have been supportive of this research endeavor, including Petra, Skyler, Sarah, Steve, Anders, my supporters on *Patreon*[4], all the friends in our social media chats, and so many who tagged me on social media to inquire on this particular area of research. You may not realize it, but you've been keeping me going.

My wife, Samantha, deserves a special thank you. I know she was bored beyond belief editing this book for me, but she did it anyways. Yes, we will finally get back to spending evenings watching that queue of TV shows that has been growing for months.

Finally, I have to give a special shoutout to my daughter, Gabriella, who stopped by my desk every evening to check on me and make sure my "research project" was progressing well.

Differences Between Editions

The Third Edition:

- Added Utah's new House Bill 113, which was ratified on March 16, 2021
- Included reference to *Kyne v. Kyne* (38 Cal. App. 2d 122, 1940) in California
- Included reference to 1997 Hawaii Revised Statutes amendment that added requirement of "medical insurance premiums"
- Reduced digital edition's file size through better image compression
- Corrected minor typos

The Second Edition:

- Added an explanation for Puerto Rico including both Spanish and English text
- Added more links to original legislation in the Hathi Trust archives
- Included earlier initial legislation for the Territory of Wisconsin, predating statehood
- Included earlier initial legislation for the Territory of Dakota, predating several states
- Included earlier initial legislation for Arkansas (1838, previously 1875)
- Corrected chapter number for 1921 Delaware session law
- Made several minor tweaks to titles of session laws

Table of Contents

Prompt to Conduct the Research	1
General History	3
Scope of Research	4
Timeline of Enactment	5
Map of Coverage	6
Alabama	7
Alaska	8
Arizona	9
Arkansas	10
California	11
Colorado	12
Connecticut	13
Delaware	14
Florida	15
Georgia	16
Hawaii	17
Idaho	18
Illinois	19
Indiana	20
Iowa	21
Kansas	22
Kentucky	23
Louisiana	24
Maine	25
Maryland	26
Massachusetts	27
Michigan	28
Minnesota	29
Mississippi	30
Missouri	31
Montana	32
Nebraska	33
Nevada	34
New Hampshire	35
New Jersey	36

New Mexico	37
New York	38
North Carolina	39
North Dakota	40
Ohio	41
Oklahoma	42
Oregon	43
Pennsylvania	44
Rhode Island	45
South Carolina	46
South Dakota	47
Tennessee	48
Texas	49
Utah	50
Vermont	51
Virginia	52
Washington	53
West Virginia	54
Wisconsin	55
Wyoming	56
District of Columbia	57
American Samoa	58
Guam	59
Northern Mariana Islands	60
Puerto Rico	61
US Virgin Islands	62
Federal	63
Endnotes	64

Prompt to Conduct the Research

My prompt to conduct the research that eventually lead to this book came in early 2019. At the time, there was a wave of legislation passing through states relating to abortion. Legislators were prompted to draft these bills by the perception that the *US Supreme Court* was shifting more conservative under the Trump Administration. The more conservative legislatures aimed to test this by drafting fetal heartbeat bills that declared (or sometimes redeclared) human rights before birth. The more progressive legislatures aimed to preemptively assert States' Rights by expanding abortion access and declaring induced abortions to be women's rights. It became obvious to me early during this legislative wave that media reports across the political spectrum were pushing agendas, rather than actually reporting what these bills contained. Thus, I decided to start reading every one of them on my own to see what they actually said.

During my readings of legislation, I eventually came to *Georgia's House Bill 481*[5], which the *General Assembly* titled the *Living Infants Fairness and Equality (LIFE) Act*. Section 5 of the Act contained an amendment to the *Official Code of Georgia Annotated*[6] that addressed "alimony and child support" for an unborn child with a detectable heartbeat.

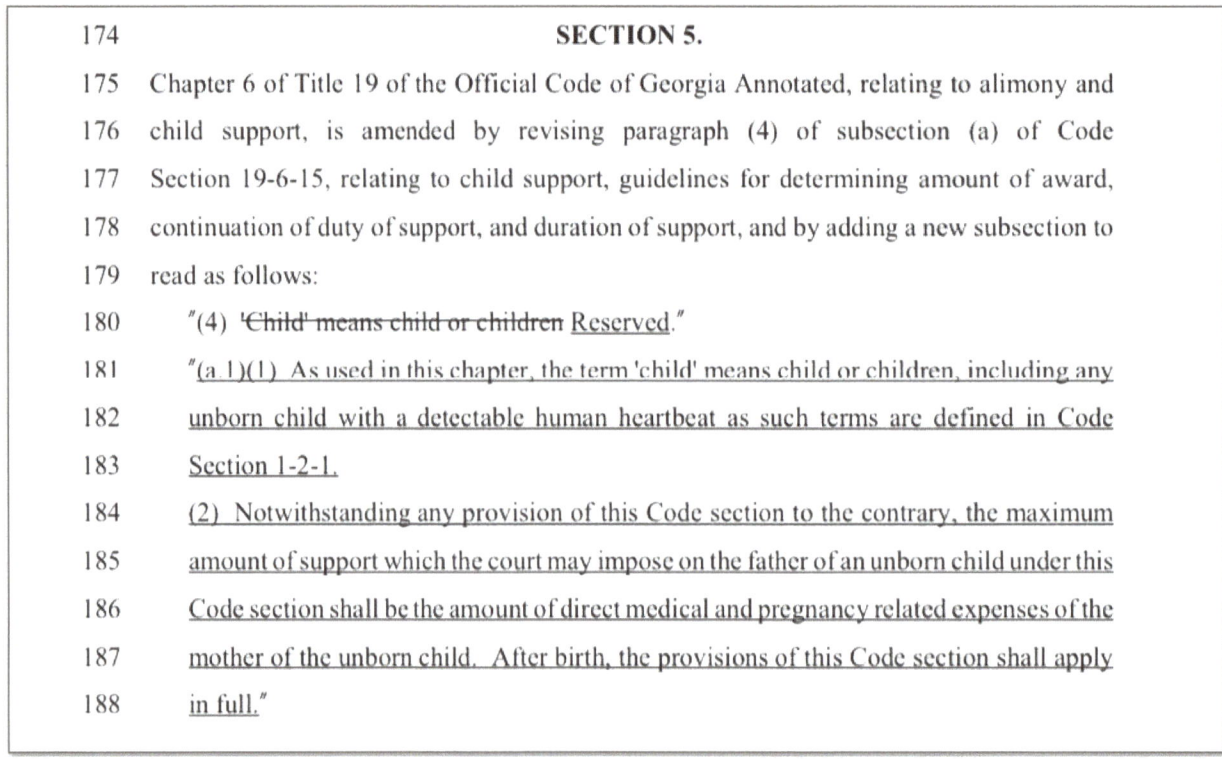

Figure 1: House Bill 481 (Ga., 2019)

Prenatal child support seemed like a completely logical concept to me. After numerous discussions on *Twitter*, in which pro-choicers and pro-lifers generally agreed that fathers should have to pay child support before birth, I decided to investigate which states had such requirements. For any states that lacked such requirements, my plan was to help, in any way I could, with a push to enact prenatal child support within them, creating template legislation from existing statutes.

Over a period of about three months, I searched through legal codes in every state and the District of Columbia to uncover existing laws and to determine the original legislation that added prenatal child support. I initially expected that, perhaps, a handful of states would have such laws, but the list continued to grow. Several states implemented what they called the *Parentage Act*[7] — with nearly identical wording — so I dug into that and discovered the *Uniform Law Commission*[8] and their template legislations from 1973, 2000, and 2017. Researching further, I found that the 2000 revision was primarily amended with references to the *United States Code*[9]. By the time this preliminary research journey reached its conclusion, I found that all fifty states and the District of Columbia already required prenatal child support. Additionally, there were Federal codes that related to reciprocity of child support between states and even other nations.

After writing an article on this research for the *Human Defense Initiative*[10], I began other research projects. During these, I came across several full state archives available online. Since the initial prenatal child support research only contained a small collection of scans from original legislation, I decided to resume the research and acquire as many scans as possible. This started with South Dakota, since a second look at the annotation under *South Dakota Codified Laws § 25-8-3*[11] seemed to indicate that the initial prenatal requirements may have actually come as early as 1939 — and only renumbered in 1984. If this was the case, South Dakota would have predated *Nebraska Revised Statutes § 43-1407*[12] (the earliest I had discovered so far) by two years. Following the legislative rabbit hole to the *South Dakota Code of 1939*[13] confirmed this. Interestingly, that 1939 code had a reference to an even earlier legal code and the *Uniform Illegitimacy Act* of 1923[14]. This completely changed the trajectory of the research, since it could mean that other states had prenatal child support laws in legal codes preceding their current ones. As I quickly discovered, this was the case in numerous states. To make matters more complicated, some states even started with new baseline codes every few decades without providing clear annotations to the earlier ones. (The second edition additionally references instances of territories having statutes before they later became states.)

This book contains the results of the research by presenting a collection of statutes and codes within the United States that relate to any requirements for a father to provide support for his unborn child. This usually comes in the form of immediately or retroactively helping to pay for pregnancy expenses of the mother or assisting her in other ways up to and through childbirth and the subsequent recovery. The laws may also go into detail about how the father must reimburse those who provided any assistance to the mother before he began providing her with support.

Where possible, I have included pages of the original legislation with yellow boxes around the applicable excerpts. These were sourced from state archives, online archives, legislature websites, or legal repositories. The remaining states and territories either had transcriptions of the original legislation or offered nothing but the derived codes, so those are included, instead. Some states had wealths of resources, so there are multiple images. In the few instances where court cases established precedent before legislation, the pages for those jurisdictions include documents relating to the cases, as well.

A few laws display trigger status or stricken status. Trigger laws only go into effect if preconditions or legal outcomes allow so. Stricken laws were generally replaced by newer ones, rather than being recodified or amended.

General History

In the early colonial era of what became the United States, it was very common for local governments and charities to care for paupers, indigents, and others who couldn't care for themselves and had no blood-relatives available to care for them. Many of the methods of implementation were inherited from English common law.

When "bastardy" and "illegitimacy" laws initially arose in the late colonial era, the courts would try to collect from the father to cover child support expenses, either by reimbursement to the local funds or as direct payments to the mothers. Most jurisdictions handled the cases in the form of criminal trials, but they were almost always quasi-civil matters in the sense that the burdens of proof were allowed to be "clear and convincing," rather than "beyond a reasonable doubt." The plaintiffs varied by state, generally being the mothers, the localities, or the states themselves. The putative fathers or their estates would be the defendants. The defendants would pay court expenses if found "guilty." The mothers would pay the expenses if paternity could not be proven.

Initially, the bastardy and illegitimacy laws took wildly different forms, but they started exhibiting commonalities as territories became new states in groups. Sometimes, the legislation included references to prenatal coverage as "lying-in expenses" or "confinement."

By the turn of the twentieth century, eleven states had requirements for the father to cover prenatal expenses in child support proceedings. With the rise of *Uniform* legislation, states continued to add prenatal requirements in blocks. The first quarter of the twentieth century saw fifteen states add prenatal support requirements, many of these specifically titling legislation as the *Uniform Illegitimacy Act*.

In the 1920s, there was a growing push to drop the terms "bastard" and "illegitimate" from the legal codes, with preference for using less offensive descriptions for the children[15]. As the decades progressed, many state legislatures replaced their applicable laws with new ones that treated the children as victims of their circumstances, focusing on the "paternity" or "parentage" aspects. Additionally, Federal-level and state-level programs began to overtake local ones, so the entire landscape relating to child support evolved.

By the late twentieth century, most states and a few territories had their own prenatal child support requirements. The final push for universality in the United States came with Federal passage of the *Personal Responsibility and Work Opportunity Reconciliation Act*[16] in 1996. This amended Title IV-D of the *Social Security Act* and provided minimum child support requirements for the entire United States, by allowing of bills for the costs of pregnancy and childbirth as evidence in paternity courts.

Scope of Research

The topic of *child support* can be very broad. Since this book focuses on the emergence of prenatal requirements in the United States, the scope stays closely to that particular subset of the overall topic. It occasionally ventures into related areas like estate liabilities, interstate reciprocity, abandonment, alimony, and court cases, to illustrate points on the evolution of prenatal child support. This book does not, however, include problems with collection, inadequacies in legal proceedings, bureaucratic nightmares, punishment for non-support, support for children conceived in rape, or the myriad of other related topics.

The book provides a look at the one specific topic of prenatal child support, something that does not appear to have had any major legal reviews in the past. It is my hope that this look at the histories for every state and territory will help to open the eyes of anyone unaware that prenatal child support is even a legal concept.

For many of the upcoming pages in the book, the reader will see the entire history of the laws per jurisdiction. In some cases, that initial law may still be the current one. In other cases, there may have been numerous intermediary legal codes that are excluded for the sake of brevity. Whatever the case, the per-jurisdiction review seeks to give an overview of the initial and the current laws in place and at least one accompanying image.

Timeline of Enactment

This timeline shows the first date in which each state or territory added prenatal child support requirements. Color-coding matches the map on the next page, though a few jurisdictions have flipped between the applicable colors as their legal codes have evolved. Pennsylvania and Kansas have ambiguous dates of initial requirements. These are explained in detail on their pages within this book.

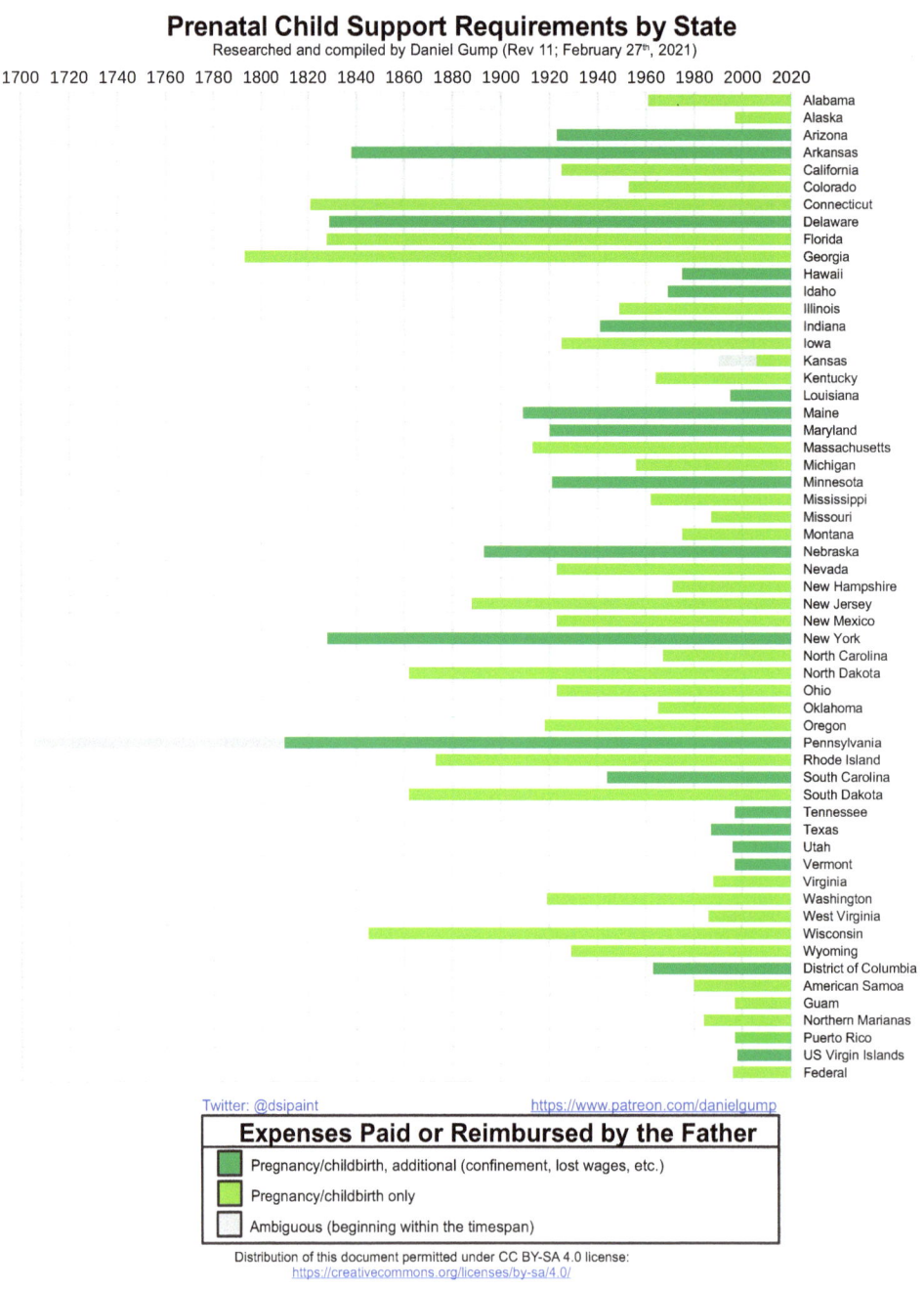

Figure 2: Prenatal Child Support Requirements by State (Timeline)

Map of Coverage

This map provides a quick overview of expected coverage in all states and territories. Pregnancy and childbirth also include "confinement" and "lying-in" where they are mentioned. Though the archaic terms can ambiguously refer to the period immediately following childbirth, states and territories in dark green specifically mention longer-term coverage as "postnatal" or "recovery." Additionally, Hawaii requires coverage for health insurance premiums, and Minnesota requires reimbursement of lost wages. Expenses relating to legal costs and genetic testing have been excluded, since they apply to child support in general.

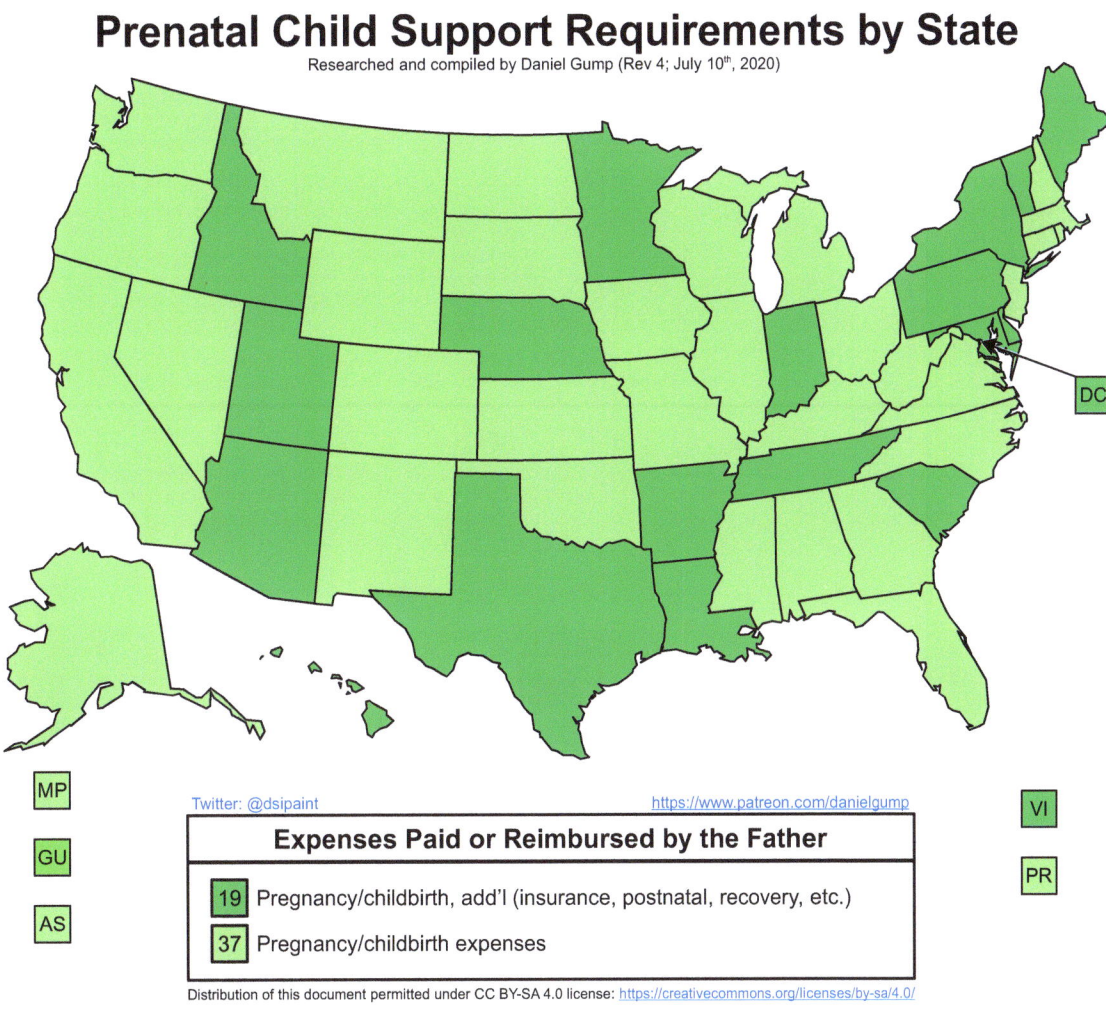

Figure 3: Prenatal Child Support Requirements by State (Map)

Alabama

Alabama Code, §26-17-636(g) *(Order adjudicating parentage; Acts 1961, ch.295 §4, amended in Acts 2008, ch.376)*
The order may direct the father to pay the **reasonable expenses of the mother's pregnancy and confinement**.

Alabama Code, §26-17-15(a) *(Effect of acknowledgment of paternity; Acts 1984, ch.84, repealed in Acts 2008, ch.376)*
~~If the existence of the father and child relationship is declared, or paternity or a duty of support has been acknowledged or adjudicated under this chapter, prior law or applicable sections of the criminal code, the obligation of the father may be enforced in the same or other proceedings by the mother, the child, the public authorities that have furnished or may **furnish the reasonable expenses of pregnancy, confinement**, education, or support, or by any other person, including a private agency, to the extent these expenses have been or are being furnished.~~

Alabama Code, §26-17-305(b) *(Effect of acknowledgment of paternity; Acts 2008, ch.376)*
An acknowledgment of paternity shall be a legally sufficient basis for establishing an obligation for child support and for the **expenses of the mother's pregnancy and confinement**.

> 2354
>
> Section 3. The Circuit Solicitor or his Deputy Circuit Solicitor or the County Solicitor, as the case may be, shall appear and prosecute all paternity proceedings brought under this Act.
>
> Section 4. If a reputed father is found guilty or admits the truth of the complaint, he shall be adjudged to be the father of such child, and thenceforth shall be subject to all obligations for the care, maintenance, and education of such child and to all the penalties for failure to perform the same which are or shall be imposed by law upon the father of a legitimate child of like age and capacity. Judgment may be for periodic payments which may vary in amount. The court may order payments to be made to the mother or other persons or agency designated to administer them under the supervision of the court. Judgment may also be entered against him for the reasonable expense of the mother's pregnancy and confinement. The court may at any time subsequent to the rendition of the original order or judgment modify or vacate any such order or judgment in proceedings brought under this act on written petition duly filed by either party to the original complaint, which petition shall set out in reasonable detail the facts and circumstances allegedly warranting such modification or vacation. Upon the filing of any such petition, reasonable notice shall be given to the other party of the filing thereof and the time and place set for hearing the same. No modification or vacation of the original judgment shall be had except on a showing of substantially changed conditions subsequent to the rendition of said original judgment.
>
> Section 5. In any illegitimacy case the Court, upon application made by the reputed father whose blood is involved, shall order the mother, child and reputed father to submit to one or more blood tests to determine whether or not the accused can be excluded as the father of the child. No such blood test of any child shall be taken before the child reaches the age of six months. Whenever the Court orders any such blood test to be taken, the mother shall refuse to submit either herself or the child to the test, such fact shall be disclosed upon the trial unless good cause is shown for not doing so. Any tests shall be made by an expert qualified as an examiner of blood types, and he shall be appointed by the Court. The Court shall fix the compensation of any expert at a reasonable amount, and may direct the same to be paid by the county or any other party to the case or by both, in such proportions and at such times as the Court shall prescribe. Prior to the making of said test, the Court may order any part or all of the said compensation paid in advance. The result of the tests shall be receivable in evi-

Figure 4: *Acts*, ch. 376 (Ala., 1961)

Alaska

Though Alaska was one of the last states to implement prenatal child support, the territorial legislature did pass the *Uniform Reciprocal Enforcement of Support Act* in 1953 (*SLA 1953* ch. 31, SB10). The purposes stated in § 1 were "to improve and extend by reciprocal legislation the enforcement of duties of support and to make uniform the law with respect thereto." It's unclear what effect this actually had in Alaska, since the majority of states had prenatal child support explicitly written at this point, meaning Alaska's absence would most likely exclude that aspect of the reciprocity in child support cases.

Alaska Statutes, 2018, §25.20.050(j) *(Legitimation by subsequent marriage, acknowledgment in writing, or adjudication; 41 ch 87 SLA 1997, SB154)*
Invoices, bills, or other standard documents showing **charges for medical and related costs of pregnancy, childbirth**, or genetic testing are admissible in an action to establish paternity without testimony or other evidence from the medical or other provider or third-party payor to provide the foundation for admissibility of the documents. The documents shall constitute prima facie evidence of the amounts incurred for such charges.

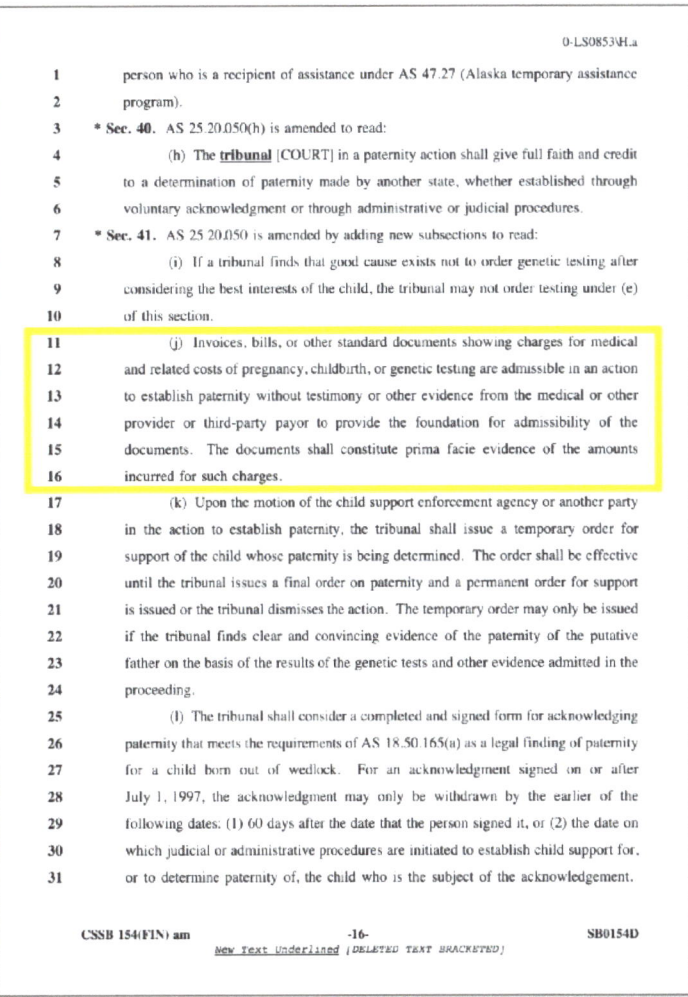

Figure 5: *41 ch.87 SLA* (Alaska, 1993)

Arizona

Revised Statutes of Arizona, 1913, Civil Code unknown section *(Bases for jurisdiction over nonresident; Laws of Arizona, 1923, ch. 72 § 3; HB101)*
If the defendant pays, or secures to be paid, to the complainant such sum of money or other property as she, with the written approval of the board of supervisors of the county, may agree to receive in full satisfaction, a memorandum of which agreement and approval the justice shall enter in his docket, and shall also pay the costs of prosecution and **the expenses incurred by such county for the lying-in and support of and attendance upon the mother during her sickness**, and give bond to the county, approved by the justice, conditioned to indemnify such county against all charges for the maintenance of the child born, or that may be born, the justice shall discharge him.

Arizona Revised Statutes, §25-1221(4) *(Bases for jurisdiction over nonresident; HB 2332, 2004)*
The individual resided in this state and provided **prenatal expenses** or support for the child.

Arizona Revised Statutes, §25-1256(D) *(Special rules of evidence and procedure; HB 2332, 2004)*
Copies of bills for testing for parentage of a child and for prenatal and postnatal health care of the mother and child furnished to the adverse party at least ten days before trial are admissible in evidence to prove the amount of the charges billed and that the charges were reasonable, necessary and customary.

LAWS OF ARIZONA 181

Section 1. On complaint being made to a justice of the peace by any woman who is delivered of a bastard child, or pregnant with a child which, if born alive, might be a bastard, accusing any person of being the father of such child, the justice shall take the complaint in writing, under her oath, and thereupon shall issue his warrant, directed to the sheriff or any constable of his county, commanding him forthwith to bring such accused person before him to answer such complaint; which warrant may be executed anywhere within this state.

Section 2. The justice shall enter an action in his docket, in which the state shall be plaintiff, and the accused defendant, and shall make such other entries as are required in criminal actions. On the return of the warrant with the accused, the justice shall examine under oath the complainant, and such other witnesses as may be produced by the parties, respecting the complaint, and shall reduce such examination to writing.

Section 3. If the defendant pays, or secures to be paid, to the complainant such sum of money or other property as she, with the written approval of the board of supervisors of the county, may agree to receive in full satisfaction, a memorandum of which agreement and approval the justice shall enter in his docket, and shall also pay the costs of prosecution and the expenses incurred by such county for the lying-in and support of and attendance upon the mother during her sickness, and give bond to the county, approved by the justice, conditioned to indemnify such county against all charges for the maintenance of the child born, or that may be born, the justice shall discharge him.

Section 4. If the defendant does not comply

Figure 6: *Laws*, ch. 72 (Ariz., 1923)

Arkansas

Arkansas' first prenatal child support law came in 1838 and saw numerous revisions, including in 1875. The state is unique in that the statute has preserved the archaic term "lying-in expenses" through 182 years of recodifications and amendments.

Arkansas Code Annotated, §9-10-110 *(Judgment for lying in expenses; Acts 1838 ch.19 § 5; Act 1875 Adj Sess ch.24 § 5, recodified several times, also split into ACA §9-10-111 for general requirements)*

(a) **If it is found by the court that the accused is the father of the child, the court shall render judgment against him for the lying-in expenses in favor of the mother, person, or agency incurring the lying-in expenses, if claimed.**

(b) **If the lying-in expenses are not paid upon the rendition of the judgment, together with all costs that may be adjudged against him in the case, then the court shall have the power to commit the accused person to jail until the lying-in expenses are paid, with all costs.**

Arkansas Code Annotated, §9-17-201(a)(4) *(Bases for jurisdiction over nonresident; Acts 1979, no.71 §1; amended in Acts 1993, ch. 468)*

the individual resided in this state and provided **prenatal expenses or support for the child**;

Arkansas Code Annotated, §9-17-316(d) *(Special rules of evidence and procedure; Acts 1979 no.71 §1; amended in Acts 1993, ch. 468)*

Copies of bills for testing for parentage of a child, and for **prenatal and postnatal health care of the mother and child,** furnished to the adverse party at least 10 days before trial, are admissible in evidence to prove the amount of the charges billed and that the charges were reasonable, necessary, and customary.

146 BASTARDY. [CHAP. XIX.

born alive, may be a bastard, charging on oath any person with being the father of such child, the justice shall issue his warrant to the sheriff, coroner or any constable of the county, commanding him forthwith to bring such accused person before him to answer such complaint.

SEC. 3. When the warrant is returned, if the child is not born, the justice shall require the person charged as the father to enter into recognizance to the State in the sum of three hundred dollars, with sufficient security, conditioned to be void if such person shall appear before said justice at the expiration of thirty days after the birth of such child, and on every subsequent day to which the justice may adjourn the case; and in case of a failure to enter into such recognizance, the justice shall commit such person to the common jail of the county.

SEC. 4. When it is determined that a person is the father of a bastard child, the justice shall order that such person with sufficient security become bound to the State of Arkansas, by a joint and several obligation, in the penal sum of three hundred dollars, with condition to be void if such person, or his executor or administrator, shall indemnify each county in the State from all costs and expenses for the maintenance or otherwise of such child while under the age of seven years.

SEC. 5. Such justice shall further order, that such person pay, for the lying-in expenses, to the mother or the person who incurred the same, a sum not less than five nor more than fifteen dollars, and for the maintenance and the support of such child, to the mother or other person keeping such child, a monthly sum, not less than one dollar nor more than three dollars for every month from the birth until the child shall attain the age of seven years.

SEC. 6. The order in the preceding section specified, shall be of the same nature as a judgment before a justice of the peace, and execution may be issued for any sum in arrear by the justice making the order, or any other justice with whom a transcript of such order may be lodged.

SEC. 7. Such order may be revived against the executor or administrator of the person against whom the same was entered, in like manner as a judgment.

SEC. 8. If such person shall refuse or neglect to enter into bond with security as required in the fourth section of this act, the justice shall commit him to the jail of the county, there to remain until he shall comply with such order, or until he shall be otherwise discharged according to law.

Figure 7: *Acts*, ch.19 § 5 (Ark., 1838)

9-10-110. Judgment for lying-in expenses — Commitment on failure to pay.

(a) If it is found by the court that the accused is the father of the child, the court shall render judgment against him for the lying-in expenses in favor of the mother, person, or agency incurring the lying-in expenses, if claimed.

(b) If the lying-in expenses are not paid upon the rendition of the judgment, together with all costs that may be adjudged against him in the case, then the court shall have the power to commit the accused person to jail until the lying-in expenses are paid, with all costs.

(c)

(1) Bills and invoices for pregnancy and childbirth expenses and paternity testing are admissible as evidence in the circuit court or juvenile division of circuit court without third-party foundation testimony if such bills or invoices are regular on their face.

(2) Such bills or invoices shall constitute prima facie evidence of amounts incurred for such services or for testing on behalf of the child.

Figure 8: *Arkansas Code,* § 9-10-110

California

California had a unique method of instituting prenatal child support. What the state legislature did in 1925 was amend *California Penal Code* §270 in relation to "Abandonment and Neglect of Children" with the text "A child conceived but not yet born is to be deemed an existing person insofar as this section is concerned." This code section was referenced in *Kyne v. Kyne* (1940)[17], among other cases, when considering judgments.

California Penal Code, §270 *(Abandonment and Neglect of Children, Statutes 1925 Ch. 325 p. 545)*
The provisions of this section are applicable whether the parents of such child are married or divorced, and regardless of any decree made in any divorce action relative to alimony or to the support of the child. **A child conceived but not yet born is to be deemed an existing person insofar as this section is concerned.**

California Family Code, §7637 *(Determination of Parent and Child Relationship; Statutes 1992, Ch. 162, Sec. 10, Div. 12, Part 3, Ch. 4, Art. 1, p. 655)*
The judgment or order may contain any other provision directed against the appropriate party to the proceeding, concerning the duty of support, the custody and guardianship of the child, visitation privileges with the child, the furnishing of bond or other security for the payment of the judgment, or any other matter in the best interest of the child. **The judgment or order may direct the parent to pay the reasonable expenses of the mother's pregnancy and confinement.**

California Family Code, §7641(a) *(Determination of Parent and Child Relationship, Statutes 1992, Ch. 162, Sec. 10, Div. 12, Part 3, Ch. 4, Art. 1, p. 656)*
If there is a voluntary declaration of paternity in place, or parentage or a duty of support has been acknowledged or adjudicated under this part or under prior law, the obligation of the parent may be enforced in the same or other proceedings by any of the following: (1) The other parent. (2) The child. (3) The public authority that has furnished or may furnish the **reasonable expenses of pregnancy, confinement**, education, support, or funeral. (4) Any other person, including a private agency, to the extent the person has furnished or is furnishing these expenses.

Figure 9: *California Statutes 1925, ch.325*

California Family Code, §7604.5 *(General provisions, Statutes 1997, Ch. 599, Sec. 44, p. 3723)*
SEC. 44. Section 7604.5 is added to the Family Code, to read:
7604.5. Notwithstanding any other provision of law, **bills for pregnancy, childbirth**, and genetic testing shall be admissible as evidence without third-party foundation testimony and shall constitute prima facie evidence of costs incurred for those services.

Colorado

Colorado seems to be unique for the modern era in that prenatal child support did not originate from legislation but from a ruling by the *Supreme Court of Colorado* in 1953. In this case, the Court ruled on constitutionality of the juvenile court "compelling the father to care for and support an unborn child and its mother." Legislation did follow forty years later, using similar language to what other states were enacting at the time.

Cederquist v. Archuleta (1953) *(127 Colo. 41, 253 P.2d 431)*
We have heretofore determined that section 1, chapter 33, supra, **compelling the father to care for and support an unborn child and its mother, is constitutional**, and have repeatedly held that the juvenile court has jurisdiction to determine the parentage of children yet unborn.

Colorado Revised Statutes, §19-4-116(3)(a) *(Judgment or order - birth related costs; Session Laws 1993, ch.165, SB 93-25)*
The judgment or order may contain any other provision directed against the appropriate party to the proceeding concerning the duty of support, the recovery of child support debt pursuant to section 14-14-104, C.R.S., the allocation of parental responsibilities with respect to the child and guardianship of the child, parenting time privileges with the child, the furnishing of bond or other security for the payment of the judgment, or any other matter in the best interest of the child. The judgment or order may direct the father to pay for genetic testing and to pay the **reasonable expenses of the mother's pregnancy and confinement.**

Colorado Revised Statutes, §19-4-116(3)(c) *(Judgment or order - birth related costs; Session Laws 1997, ch.236, HB 97-1205)*
Bills for pregnancy, childbirth expenses, and genetic testing are admissible as evidence without the necessity of third-party foundation testimony and shall constitute prima facie evidence of the amounts incurred for such services or for expenses incurred on behalf of the child.

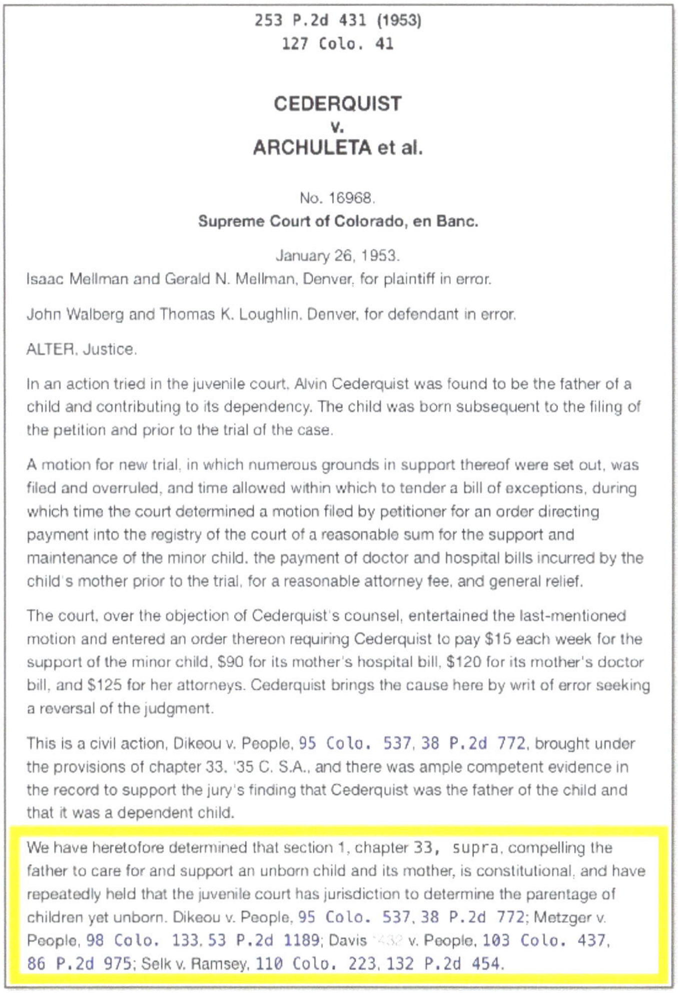
253 P.2d 431 (1953)
127 Colo. 41

CEDERQUIST
v.
ARCHULETA et al.

No. 16968.
Supreme Court of Colorado, en Banc.

January 26, 1953.

Isaac Mellman and Gerald N. Mellman, Denver, for plaintiff in error.

John Walberg and Thomas K. Loughlin, Denver, for defendant in error.

ALTER, Justice.

In an action tried in the juvenile court, Alvin Cederquist was found to be the father of a child and contributing to its dependency. The child was born subsequent to the filing of the petition and prior to the trial of the case.

A motion for new trial, in which numerous grounds in support thereof were set out, was filed and overruled, and time allowed within which to tender a bill of exceptions, during which time the court determined a motion filed by petitioner for an order directing payment into the registry of the court of a reasonable sum for the support and maintenance of the minor child, the payment of doctor and hospital bills incurred by the child's mother prior to the trial, for a reasonable attorney fee, and general relief.

The court, over the objection of Cederquist's counsel, entertained the last-mentioned motion and entered an order thereon requiring Cederquist to pay $15 each week for the support of the minor child, $90 for its mother's hospital bill, $120 for its mother's doctor bill, and $125 for her attorneys. Cederquist brings the cause here by writ of error seeking a reversal of the judgment.

This is a civil action, Dikeou v. People, 95 Colo. 537, 38 P.2d 772, brought under the provisions of chapter 33, '35 C. S.A., and there was ample competent evidence in the record to support the jury's finding that Cederquist was the father of the child and that it was a dependent child.

We have heretofore determined that section 1, chapter 33, supra, compelling the father to care for and support an unborn child and its mother, is constitutional, and have repeatedly held that the juvenile court has jurisdiction to determine the parentage of children yet unborn. Dikeou v. People, 95 Colo. 537, 38 P.2d 772; Metzger v. People, 98 Colo. 133, 53 P.2d 1189; Davis *432 v. People, 103 Colo. 437, 86 P.2d 975; Selk v. Ramsey, 110 Colo. 223, 132 P.2d 454.

Figure 10: *Cederquist v. Archuleta* (127 Colo. 41, 1953)

Connecticut

Connecticut's first prenatal child support legislation came in 1821, as an amendment to the colonial "Bastardy and Fornication" law from 1702. The *Acts and Laws of His Majesties Colony of Connecticut in New England* that contains the law is noteworthy for its inclusion of decorative headings, the use of the archaic long "s" (ſ), and a notation added to the beginning of the digitized copy that this was the rarest revision of all printed colonial Connecticut laws.

General Statutes, §19-17-3-3 *(Bastardy, Judgment; Session Laws 1821 title 8; seen in 1875 General Statutes edition)*
And if the court find him guilty, they shall make an order, that he shall stand charged with the maintenance of such child, with the assistance of the. mother, and that he shall pay a certain sum per week, for such time as the court shall judge proper, and that the clerk of the court shall issue execution for the same, quarterly : and **the court shall ascertain the expence of lying-in**, and the nursing of such child, till the time of rendering judgment, and order him to pay one half thereof to the complainant, and grant execution for the same, and lawful cost of suit :

Figure 11: *Acts* (Conn., 1702)

General Statutes, §46b-172a(a) *(Filing of claim for paternity by putative father; Public Acts 1990, ch.31 §8)*
...The claim for paternity shall be admissible in any action for paternity under section 46b-160, and shall estop the claimant from denying his paternity of such child and shall contain language that he acknowledges liability for contribution to the support and education of the child after the child's birth and for contribution to the **pregnancy-related medical expenses of the mother**.

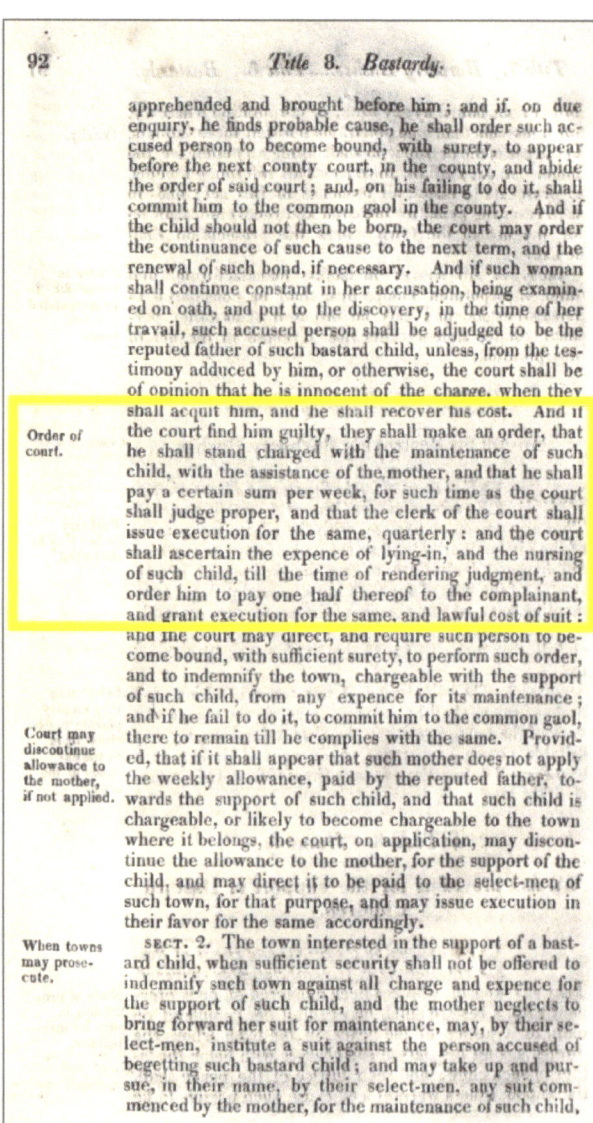

Figure 12: *Session Laws*, Title 8 (Conn., 1821)

Delaware

Delaware's law went through several minor revisions over the years. Most amendments for nearly a century were little more than updates to costs for the support and court proceedings. The *Delaware Revised Statutes 1874* book I encountered actually had such revisions handwritten in it. Be aware that for the online transcription of the 1974 Session Law, there is a typo that incorrectly labels § 504 as § 501.

Unknown code section *(An act concerning bastard children; Session Laws 1829, Ch. CXVIII, §1; eventually Revised Statutes 1852 §11:77)*
...and the said justice shall further order, that the said person **pay, for the lying-in expenses, to the mother or other person, who incurred the same, a sum not less than four, not more than six, dollars** and, for the maintenance of the child, to the mother or other person keeping it a monthly sum not less than one dollar not more than two dollars every calendar month from the birth, until the child shall attain the age of seven years if so long chargeable...

Revised Code, §88-3077 *(Illegitimate children; Session Laws 1921, ch.184, §3)*
...In addition thereto the justice hearing the case shall make an order requiring the defendant to **pay the mother of the child a sum certain for lying in expenses not less than twenty-five nor more than forty dollars, and also a certain sum to the physician who attended the mother during her delivery not less than twenty nor more than thirty dollars**. All orders made shall be in the discretion of the justice, having regard to the circumstances and to the financial ability or earning power of the defendant...

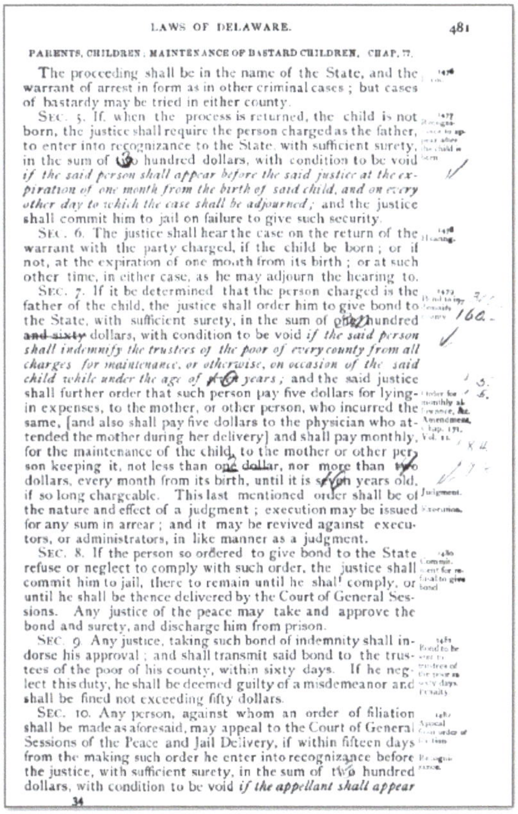

LAWS OF DELAWARE. 481

PARENTS, CHILDREN; MAINTENANCE OF BASTARD CHILDREN. CHAP. 77.

The proceeding shall be in the name of the State, and the warrant of arrest in form as in other criminal cases; but cases of bastardy may be tried in either county.

SEC. 5. If, when the process is returned, the child is not born, the justice shall require the person charged as the father, to enter into recognizance to the State, with sufficient surety, in the sum of two hundred dollars, with condition to be void *if the said person shall appear before the said justice at the expiration of one month from the birth of said child, and on every other day to which the case shall be adjourned;* and the justice shall commit him to jail on failure to give such security.

SEC. 6. The justice shall hear the case on the return of the warrant with the party charged, if the child be born; or if not, at the expiration of one month from its birth; or at such other time, in either case, as he may adjourn the hearing to.

SEC. 7. If it be determined that the person charged is the father of the child, the justice shall order him to give bond to the State, with sufficient surety, in the sum of one hundred and sixty dollars, with condition to be void *if the said person shall indemnify the trustees of the poor of every county from all charges for maintenance, or otherwise, on occasion of the said child while under the age of seven years;* and the said justice shall further order that such person pay five dollars for lying-in expenses, to the mother, or other person, who incurred the same, [and also shall pay five dollars to the physician who attended the mother during her delivery] and shall pay monthly, for the maintenance of the child, to the mother or other person keeping it, not less than one dollar, nor more than two dollars, every month from its birth, until it is seven years old, if so long chargeable. This last mentioned order shall be of the nature and effect of a judgment; execution may be issued for any sum in arrear; and it may be revived against executors, or administrators, in like manner as a judgment.

SEC. 8. If the person so ordered to give bond to the State refuse or neglect to comply with such order, the justice shall commit him to jail, there to remain until he shall comply, or until he shall be thence delivered by the Court of General Sessions. Any justice of the peace may take and approve the bond and surety, and discharge him from prison.

SEC. 9. Any justice, taking such bond of indemnity shall indorse his approval; and shall transmit said bond to the trustees of the poor of his county, within sixty days. If he neglect this duty, he shall be deemed guilty of a misdemeanor and shall be fined not exceeding fifty dollars.

SEC. 10. Any person, against whom an order of filiation shall be made as aforesaid, may appeal to the Court of General Sessions of the Peace and Jail Delivery, if within fifteen days from the making such order he enter into recognizance before the justice, with sufficient surety, in the sum of two hundred dollars, with condition to be void *if the appellant shall appear*

34

Figure 13: Delaware *Revised Statutes 1874*

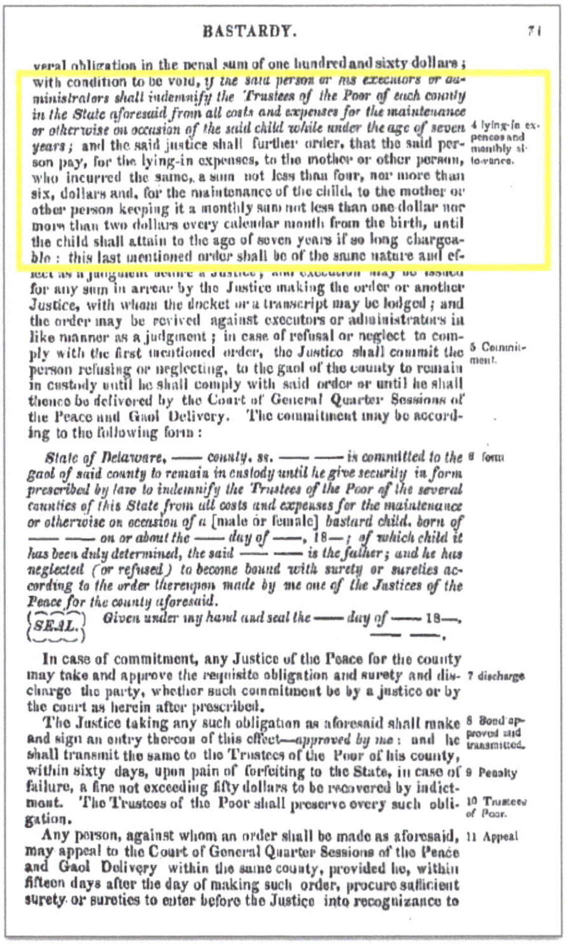

BASTARDY. 71

veral obligation in the penal sum of one hundred and sixty dollars; with condition to be void, *if the said person or his executors or administrators shall indemnify the Trustees of the Poor of each county in the State aforesaid from all costs and expenses for the maintenance or otherwise on occasion of the said child while under the age of seven years;* and the said justice shall further order, that the said person pay, for the lying-in expenses, to the mother or other person, who incurred the same, a sum not less than four, nor more than six, dollars and, for the maintenance of the child, to the mother or other person keeping it a monthly sum not less than one dollar nor more than two dollars every calendar month from the birth, until the child shall attain to the age of seven years if so long chargeable: this last mentioned order shall be of the same nature and effect as a judgment before a Justice; and execution may be issued for any sum in arrear by the Justice making the order or another Justice, with whom the docket or a transcript may be lodged; and the order may be revived against executors or administrators in like manner as a judgment; in case of refusal or neglect to comply with the first mentioned order, the Justice shall commit the person refusing or neglecting, to the gaol of the county to remain in custody until he shall comply with said order or until he shall thence be delivered by the Court of General Quarter Sessions of the Peace and Gaol Delivery. The commitment may be according to the following form: (4 lying-in expences and monthly allowance. 5 Commitment.)

State of Delaware, —— county, ss. —— —— is committed to the gaol of said county to remain in custody until he give security in form prescribed by law to indemnify the Trustees of the Poor of the several counties of this State from all costs and expenses for the maintenance or otherwise on occasion of a [male or female] *bastard child, born of —— —— on or about the —— day of ——, 18—; of which child it has been duly determined, the said —— —— is the father; and he has neglected (or refused) to become bound with surety or sureties according to the order thereupon made by me one of the Justices of the Peace for the county aforesaid.* (6 form)

(SEAL.) *Given under my hand and seal the —— day of —— 18—.*
—— ——.

In case of commitment, any Justice of the Peace for the county may take and approve the requisite obligation and surety and discharge the party, whether such commitment be by a justice or by the court as herein after prescribed. (7 discharge)

The Justice taking any such obligation as aforesaid shall make and sign an entry thereon of this effect—*approved by me*: and he shall transmit the same to the Trustees of the Poor of his county, within sixty days, upon pain of forfeiting to the State, in case of failure, a fine not exceeding fifty dollars to be recovered by indictment. The Trustees of the Poor shall preserve every such obligation. (8 Bond approved and transmitted. 9 Penalty 10 Trustees of Poor.)

Any person, against whom an order shall be made as aforesaid, may appeal to the Court of General Quarter Sessions of the Peace and Gaol Delivery within the same county, provided he, within fifteen days after the day of making such order, procure sufficient surety or sureties to enter before the Justice into recognizance to (11 Appeal)

Figure 14: *Session Laws (Del., 1829)*

Delaware Code, §13-504 *(Duty to support woman with child conceived out of wedlock; 59 Del. Laws c.567, 1974; HB334)*
The duty to support a woman pregnant with child conceived out of wedlock rests first upon the person by whom she became pregnant. Such support may include her necessary **prenatal and postnatal medical, hospital, and lying-in expenses incident to the pregnancy and to the birth of the child**, and such other relief as to the court shall seem reasonable.

Delaware Code, §13-1326 *(Relative to medical expenses incident to birth of illegitimate child; 50 Del. Laws c.454, 1955, repealed by 59 Del. Laws c.567, 1974; HB334)*
~~If it be determined that the person charged is the father of the child, said person shall be liable for the support of said child under the provisions of Chapter 5 of this Title. In addition to any order for support, the Judge may also order the defendant to pay into the Court such sums, in such installments, as to the Court, having regard to all the circumstances, shall seem proper for the purpose of **covering the medical expenses incident to the pregnancy of the mother**; and/or the medical and lying-in expenses incident to the delivery of said child, and may punish the defendant for contempt if he shall fail or refuse, without just cause, to obey the Court's order in this behalf.~~

Florida

When I came across Florida's online archives, the 1959 legislation was the oldest I could find at the time by tracking back through history of *current* state codes. Referring to their legislation as "An act related to bastardy" seemed very odd by today's standards, but it was very common terminology until the mid-twentieth century. As I later browsed through older legislation, I encountered "A[n] Act To provide for the support and maintenance of bastard children," which was enacted by the Territory of Florida in 1828. This did not require the father to cover all the prenatal expenses expected in 1959, but he was to pay "all necessary incidental expenses attending the birth of said child."

Compiled Laws, 1914, § 2-2600 *(Judgement against defendant; Acts 1827-8, §3, p.33)*
Be it farther enacted. That if the issue be found against the defendant or reputed father, then he shall be condemned, by the judgment of said court, to pay not exceeding fifty dollars, and **all necessary incidental expenses attending the birth of said child**, at the discretion of said court, yearly, for ten years, towards the support, maintenance and education of said child;

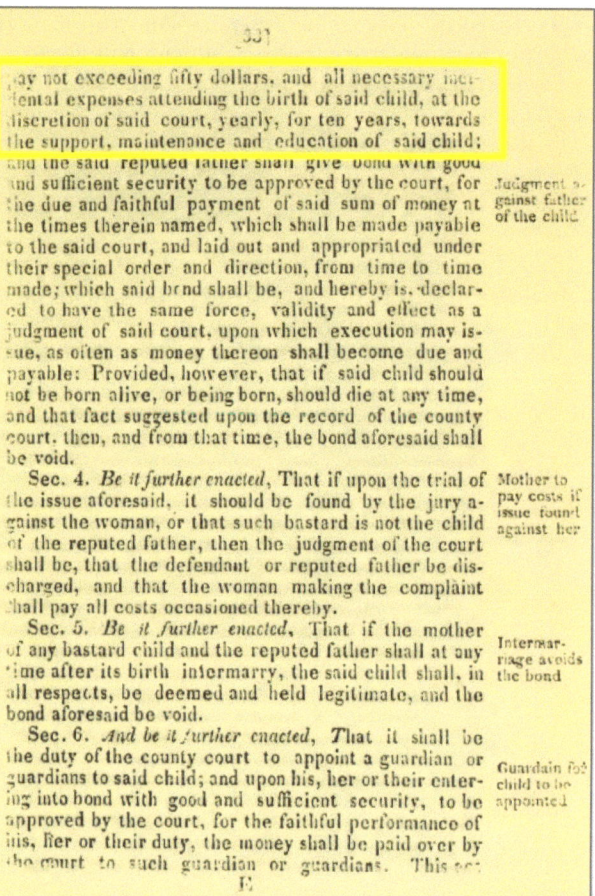

Figure 15: *Acts*, p.33 (Fla., 1827-8)

Florida Statutes, §742.031(1) *(Determination of Parentage; Laws 1951, ch.26949 §3; SB357; several later amendments)*
...If the court finds that the alleged father is the father of the child, it shall so order. If appropriate, the court shall order the father to pay the complainant, her guardian, or any other person assuming responsibility for the child moneys sufficient to pay reasonable attorney's fees, **hospital or medical expenses, cost of confinement, and any other expenses incident to the birth of the child** and to pay all costs of the proceeding. **Bills for pregnancy, childbirth**, and scientific testing are admissible as evidence without requiring third-party foundation testimony, and shall constitute prima facie evidence of amounts incurred for such services or for testing on behalf of the child...

Figure 16: *Laws*, ch.26949 (Fla., 1951)

Georgia

It was Section 5 of Georgia's *Living Infants Fairness and Equality Act* (2019)[18] that prompted this entire research project. I quickly discovered that this legislation amended just one of multiple references to prenatal child support in the *Official Code of Georgia Annotated*. Thanks to *1851 Cobb's Digest*[19], I later discovered that Georgia was actually the first state to enact prenatal child support requirements! This original legislation came in 1793 and contained some of the most-detailed requirements of any such legislation for several decades.

Unknown section *(Bastardy;* [Acts 1793]*, Vol I. ch. 42)*
...which being done, the said Justice shall issue his warrant in like manner, to bring before him the person sworn to be the father of such child or children, so born or to be born, who, on refusing to give security for the maintainance and education of such child or children, until they arrive at the age of fourteen years, **and also the expense of lying-in with such child or children, boarding, nursing, and maintainance, while the mother of such child is confined by reason thereof**, that then it may and shall be lawful for the said Justice to bind over such delinquent in a sufficient recognizance, to be and appear before the next Superior Court, which may be held in said County ;

Georgia Code 1933, statute at-large *(Uniform Support of Dependents Act, jurisdiction and powers of court;* [Ga.L. 1951]*, No.124 sec.4(b) p.111; HB33)*
The court of the responding State shall have the power to order the respondent to pay sums sufficient to provide necessary food, shelter, clothing, care, medical or hospital expenses, **expenses of confinement**, expenses of education of a child, funeral expenses and such other reasonable and proper expenses of the petitioner as justice requires, having due regard to the circumstances of the respective parties.

Georgia Code 1933, § 74-9902(d) *(Abandonment of child;* [Ga.L. 1980]*, p.1374; HB 390, replaced entire section)*
In prosecutions under this section, when the child is illegitimate, and the accused father is convicted, the accused father shall be required by the court to pay the reasonable medical **expenses paid by or incurred on behalf of the mother due to the birth of the child**.

[Official Code of Georgia Annotated], §19-6-15(a.1)(2) *(Child support guidelines for determining amount of award;* [HB 481, 2019]*; trigger law)*
Notwithstanding any provision of this Code section to the contrary, the maximum amount of support which the court may impose on the father of an unborn child under this Code section shall be the amount of **direct medical and pregnancy related expenses of the mother of the unborn child**. After birth, the provisions of this Code section shall apply in full.

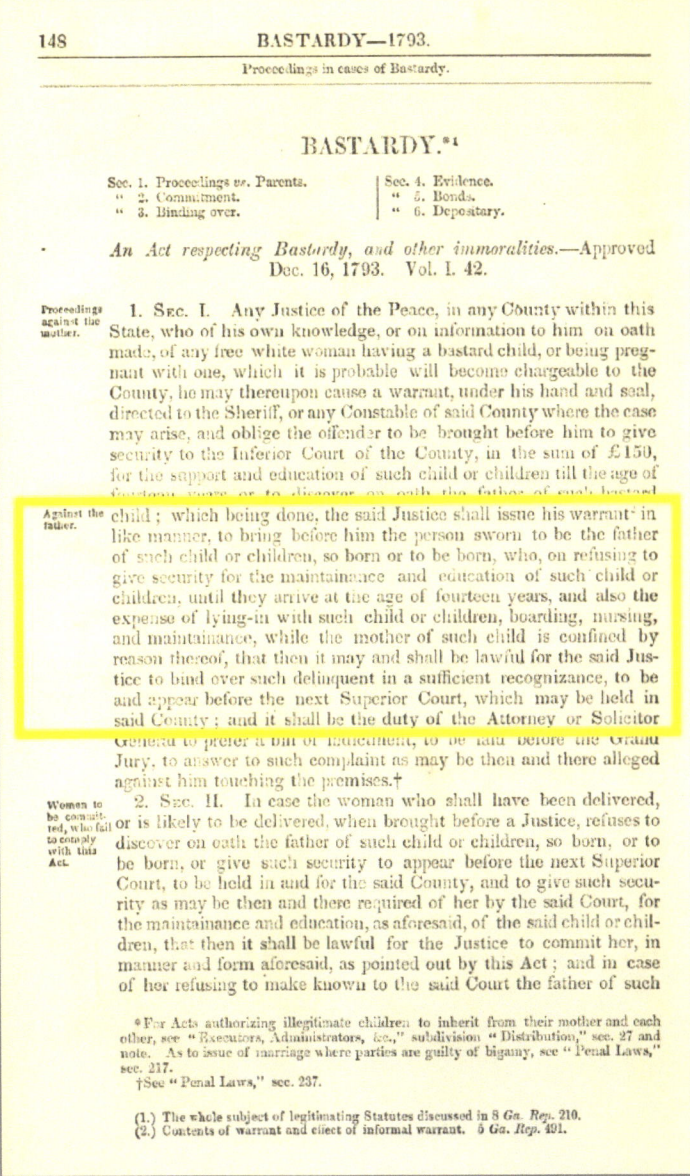

Figure 17: *Acts*, vol I, ch.42 (Ga., 1793)

[Official Code of Georgia Annotated], §19-7-49(c) *(Determination of paternity, final order;* [Ga.L. 1997]*, p.1613; HB 284, replaced previous subsection with Title IV-D compliant text, previous revision inherited from Georgia Code 1933 §74-9902(d))*
The trier of fact shall receive without foundation or the need for third-party testimony evidence of **costs of pregnancy, child birth**, and genetic testing. The evidence so presented shall constitute prima-facie evidence of amounts incurred for such services or for testing on behalf of the child. The court may award such costs as part of its final decree.

Hawaii

Hawaii Revised Statutes, §584-15(c) *(Judgment or order; Act 66, 1975, amended in Act 294, 1997 to add "medical insurance premiums)*

..The judgment or order may direct the father to pay the **reasonable expenses of the mother's pregnancy and confinement, including but not limited to medical insurance premiums**, such as for MedQuest, which cover the periods of pregnancy, childbirth, and confinement. The court may further order the noncustodial parent to reimburse the custodial parent, the child, or any public agency for reasonable expenses incurred prior to entry of judgment, including support, maintenance, education, and funeral expenses expended for the benefit of the child.

Hawaii Revised Statutes, §584-17(a) *(Enforcement of judgement or order; Act 66, 1975)*

If existence of the father and child relationship is declared, or paternity or a duty of support has been acknowledged or adjudicated under this chapter or under prior law, the obligation of the father may be enforced in the same or other proceedings by the mother, the child, the public authority that has furnished or may furnish the **reasonable expenses of pregnancy, confinement**, education, support, or funeral, or by any other person, including a private agency, to the extent the person has furnished or is furnishing these expenses.

ACT 66

der section -23.

(c) The judgment or order may contain any other provision directed against the appropriate party to the proceeding, concerning the duty of support, the custody and guardianship of the child, visitation privileges with the child, the furnishing of bond or other security for the payment of the judgment, or any other matter in the best interest of the child. Upon neglect or refusal to give such security, or upon default of the father or his surety in compliance with the terms of the judgment, the court may order the forfeiture of any such security and the application of the proceeds thereof toward the payment of any sums due under the terms of the judgment and may also sequester the father's personal estate, and the rents and profits of his real estate, and may appoint a receiver thereof, and may cause the father's personal estate, including any salaries, wages, commissions, or other moneys owed to him and the rents and profits of his real estate, to be applied toward the meeting of the terms of the judgment, to the extent that the court, from time to time, deems just and reasonable. The judgment or order may direct the father to pay the reasonable expenses of the mother's pregnancy and confinement.

(d) Support judgment or orders ordinarily shall be for periodic payments which may vary in amount. In the best interest of the child, a lump sum payment or the purchase of an annuity may be ordered in lieu of periodic payments of support. The court may limit the father's liability for past support of the child to the proportion of the expenses already incurred that the court deems just.

(e) In determining the amount to be paid by a parent for support of the child and the period during which the duty of support is owed, a court enforcing the obligation of support shall consider all relevant facts, including:

(1) The needs of the child;
(2) The standard of living and circumstances of the parents;
(3) The relative financial means of the parents;
(4) The earning ability of the parents;
(5) The need and capacity of the child for education, including higher education;
(6) The age of the child;
(7) The financial resources and the earning ability of the child;
(8) The responsibility of the parents for the support of others; and
(9) The value of services contributed by the custodial parent.

Sec. -16 Costs. The court may order reasonable fees of counsel, experts, and the child's guardian ad litem, and other costs of the action and pretrial proceedings, including blood tests, to be paid by the parties in proportions and at times determined by the court. The court may order the proportion of any indigent party to be paid by the State, or such person as the court shall direct.

Sec. -17 Enforcement of judgment or order. (a) If existence of the father and child relationship is declared, or paternity or a duty of support has been acknowledged or adjudicated under this chapter or under prior law, the obligation of the father may be enforced in the same or other proceedings by the mother, the child, the public authority that has furnished or may furnish

121

ACT 66

the reasonable expenses of pregnancy, confinement, education, support, or funeral, or by any other person, including a private agency, to the extent he has furnished or is furnishing these expenses.

(b) The court may order support payments to be made to the mother, the clerk of the court, or a person, corporation, or agency designated to administer them for the benefit of the child under the supervision of the court.

(c) Wilful failure to obey the judgment or order of the court shall be a civil contempt of the court. All remedies for the enforcement of judgments shall apply to this chapter.

Sec. -18 Modification of judgment or order. The court shall have con-

Figure 18: *Acts 66* (Hawaii, 1975)

Idaho

Since Idaho was briefly part of the Territory of Dakota, the 1862 bastardy legislation technically qualifies as the earliest. However, the resulting statute did not carry over to the Territory of Idaho, nor was there any mention of prenatal requirement in any child support legislation for over a century. Thus, as its own entity, Idaho gained requirements in 1969.

Idaho Statutes, §7-1121(2) *(Proceedings to establish paternity; Session Laws 1969, ch.93 § 20, SB1066)*
The order of filiation may direct the father to pay or reimburse amounts paid for the support of the child prior to the date of the order of filiation and may also direct him to pay or reimburse amounts paid for: (a) the funeral expenses if the child has died; (b) the necessary expenses incurred by or for the mother in connection with **her confinement and recovery**; and (c) such expenses in connection with the **pregnancy of the mother** as the court may deem proper.

C. 93 '69 IDAHO SESSION LAWS 323

SECTION 17. If the court finds that the conclusions of all the experts, as disclosed by the evidence based upon the tests, are that the defendant is not the father of the child, the question of paternity shall be resolved accordingly, and the action shall be dismissed with costs awarded to the defendant. If the experts disagree in their findings or conclusions, the action shall proceed.

SECTION 18. The presumption of legitimacy of a child born during wedlock is overcome if the court finds that the conclusions of all the experts, as disclosed by the evidence based upon the tests, show that the husband is not the father of the child.

SECTION 19. If the court finds the defendant is the father of the child, it shall make an order of filiation, declaring paternity.

SECTION 20. In a proceeding in which the court has made an order of filiation, the court shall direct a father possessed of sufficient means or able to earn such means to pay monthly or at other fixed periods a fair and reasonable sum for the support and education of the child until the child is eighteen (18) years of age. If the child continues his formal education subsequent to reaching the age of eighteen (18) years, the court may, in its discretion, order the continuation of support payments until the child discontinues his education or reaches the age of twenty-one (21) years, whichever is sooner.

The order of filiation may direct the father to pay or reimburse amounts paid for the support of the child prior to the date of the order of filiation and may also direct him to pay or reimburse amounts paid for: (1) the funeral expenses if the child has died; (2) the necessary expenses incurred by or for the mother in connection with her confinement and recovery; and (3) such expenses in connection with the pregnancy of the mother as the court may deem proper.

SECTION 21. (1) The court may require the payment to be made to the mother or to some person or corporation designated by the court as trustee. If the child is or is likely to become a public charge on a county or city, the public assistance official of that county or city shall be designated as

Figure 19: *Session Laws*, ch.93 (Idaho, 1969)

Illinois

Illinois' *General Assembly* first added a requirement for "expenses of confinement" in the *Uniform Support of Dependents Law* in 1949[20]. Since the term "confinement" by itself has fallen from use in recent decades, I looked into the amendments of this code section for later clarification. The 1967 amendment cited in *Public Acts 79-474* (1975)[21] had an additional reference to "confinement expenses of the mother or the child support payments". From the clear separation between prenatal and postnatal, it seems that the "expenses of confinement" requirement in 1949 did, in fact, have the intent of covering pregnancy.

Public Assistance Code, p.2539 *(Uniform Support of Dependents Law , Jurisdiction and powers of court, §4(b), 1949, HB869)*
~~The court of the responding state shall have the power to order the respondent to pay sums sufficient to provide necessary food, shelter, clothing, care, medical or hospital expenses,~~ **expenses of confinement**, ~~expenses of education of a child, funeral expenses and such other reasonable and proper expenses of the petitioner as justice requires, having due regard to the circumstances of the respective parties.~~

Illinois Compiled Statutes 720 § 45/9(c) *(Definitions; PA 84-848, HB 2781, 1984; repealed in 1999)*
~~The summons that is served on a defendant shall include the return date on or by which the defendant must appear and shall contain the following information, in a prominent place and in conspicuous language, in addition to the information required to be provided by the laws of this State: "If you do not appear as instructed in this summons, you may be required to support the child named in this petition until the child is at least 18 years old.~~ **You may also have to pay the pregnancy and delivery costs of the mother.**"

Illinois Compiled Statutes, 720 § 28/15(a)(3) *(Definitions; PA 95-331, HB 1531, 2015)*
payment or reimbursement of the expenses of **pregnancy and delivery** (for orders for support entered under the Illinois Parentage Act of 1984 or its predecessor the Paternity Act or under the Illinois Parentage Act of 2015)

Illinois Compiled Statutes, 720 § 46/802(b) *(Judgment; PA 95-331, HB 1531, 2015)*
In an action brought within 2 years after a child's birth, the judgment or order may direct either parent to pay the reasonable expenses incurred by either parent or the Department of Healthcare and Family Services related to the mother's **pregnancy and the delivery** of the child.

Illinois Compiled Statutes, 720 § 46/813 *(Support payments; receiving and disbursing agents; PA 95-331, HB 1531, 2015)*
(a) In an action filed in a county with less than 3,000,000 inhabitants in which an order for child support is entered, and in supplementary proceedings to enforce or vary the terms of the order arising out of an action filed in such a county, the court, except in actions or supplementary proceedings in which the **pregnancy and delivery expenses** of the mother or the child support payments are for a recipient of aid under the Illinois Public Aid Code...
(b) In an action filed in a county of 3,000,000 or more inhabitants in which an order for child support is entered, and in supplementary proceedings to enforce or vary the terms of the order arising out of an action filed in such a county, the court, except in actions or supplementary proceedings in which the **pregnancy and delivery expenses** of the mother or the child support payments are for a recipient of aid under the Illinois Public Aid Code...
(c) When the action or supplementary proceeding is on behalf of a mother for **pregnancy and delivery expenses** or for child support, or both, and the mother, child, or both, are recipients of aid under the Illinois Public Aid Code, the court shall order that the payments be made directly to...

Figure 20: HB869 (Ill., 1949)

Indiana

Indiana Code, §31-4-1-4 *(Recovery from father for prenatal and postnatal expenses; Acts 1941, ch.112, §4, H60; Repealed in Acts 1978, PL 136, §57)*
~~Obligation of Father to Mother. The mother may recover from the father the **necessary expenses of the pregnancy and birth, including but not limited to the following items: prenatal care of the mother, delivery, hospitalization**, postnatal care; and funeral expenses may be recovered should the mother die as a result of the pregnancy.~~

Indiana Code, §31-14-17-1 *(Expenses of mother's pregnancy and childbirth; Acts 1979, PL277, §1 as IC §31-6-61-17; renumbered in PL 1-1997, §6)*
The court shall order the father to pay **at least fifty percent (50%) of the reasonable and necessary expenses of the mother's pregnancy and childbirth, including the cost of: (1) prenatal care; (2) delivery; (3) hospitalization; and (4) postnatal care**.

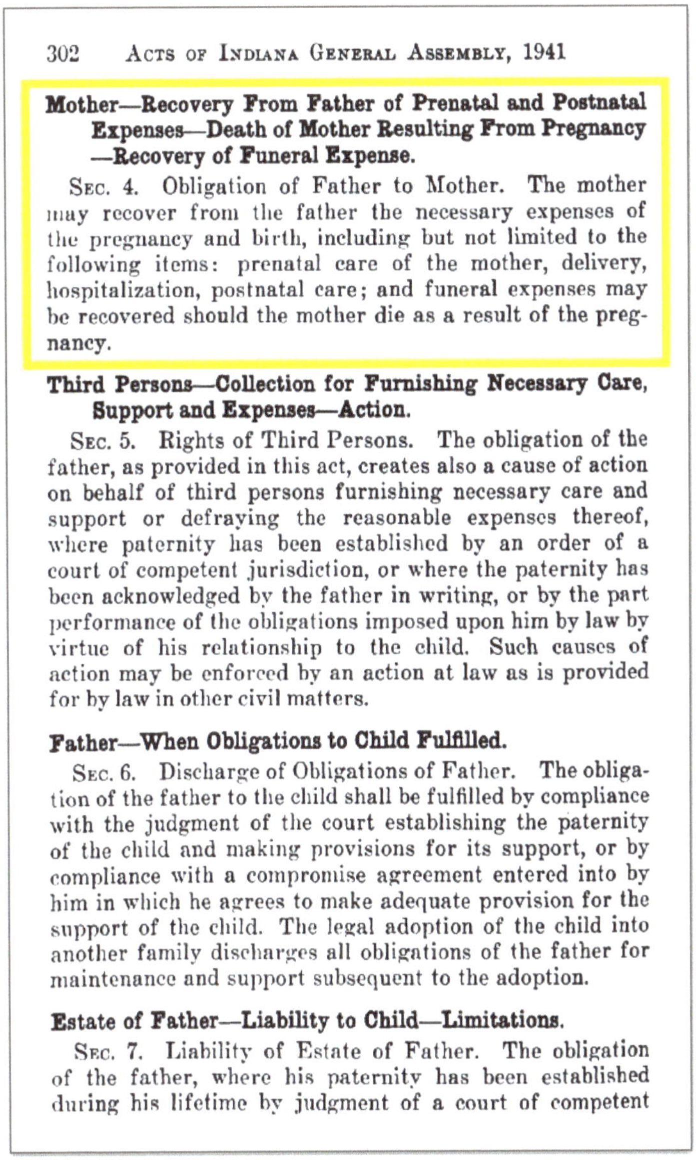

302 ACTS OF INDIANA GENERAL ASSEMBLY, 1941

Mother—Recovery From Father of Prenatal and Postnatal Expenses—Death of Mother Resulting From Pregnancy —Recovery of Funeral Expense.

SEC. 4. Obligation of Father to Mother. The mother may recover from the father the necessary expenses of the pregnancy and birth, including but not limited to the following items: prenatal care of the mother, delivery, hospitalization, postnatal care; and funeral expenses may be recovered should the mother die as a result of the pregnancy.

Third Persons—Collection for Furnishing Necessary Care, Support and Expenses—Action.

SEC. 5. Rights of Third Persons. The obligation of the father, as provided in this act, creates also a cause of action on behalf of third persons furnishing necessary care and support or defraying the reasonable expenses thereof, where paternity has been established by an order of a court of competent jurisdiction, or where the paternity has been acknowledged by the father in writing, or by the part performance of the obligations imposed upon him by law by virtue of his relationship to the child. Such causes of action may be enforced by an action at law as is provided for by law in other civil matters.

Father—When Obligations to Child Fulfilled.

SEC. 6. Discharge of Obligations of Father. The obligation of the father to the child shall be fulfilled by compliance with the judgment of the court establishing the paternity of the child and making provisions for its support, or by compliance with a compromise agreement entered into by him in which he agrees to make adequate provision for the support of the child. The legal adoption of the child into another family discharges all obligations of the father for maintenance and support subsequent to the adoption.

Estate of Father—Liability to Child—Limitations.

SEC. 7. Liability of Estate of Father. The obligation of the father, where his paternity has been established during his lifetime by judgment of a court of competent

Figure 21: *Acts*, ch.112 (Ind., 1941)

Iowa

The current prenatal child support requirements in the *Iowa Code of 2015*[22] are identical to those enacted for the *Iowa Code of 1924*[23] in 1925.

Iowa Code of 2015, §600B.1 *(Obligation of parents; originally enacted under "Paternity" in Acts 1925, ch.81, sec.1; SF138 as Code of 1924 §12667.01; newest revision under Acts 2015, ch.14, sec.2; SF223)*
The parents of a child born out of wedlock and not legitimized (in this chapter referred to as "the child") owe the child necessary maintenance, education, and support. They are also liable for the child's funeral expenses. The father is also liable to pay the **expense of the mother's pregnancy and confinement**.

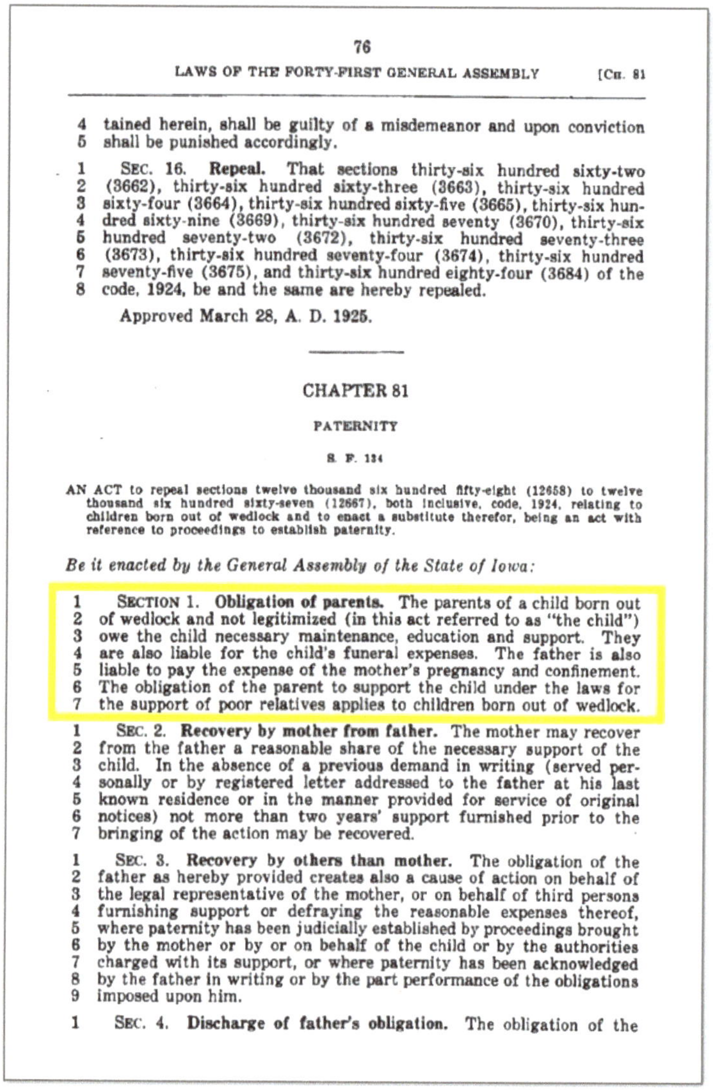

76

LAWS OF THE FORTY-FIRST GENERAL ASSEMBLY [CH. 81

tained herein, shall be guilty of a misdemeanor and upon conviction shall be punished accordingly.

SEC. 16. **Repeal.** That sections thirty-six hundred sixty-two (3662), thirty-six hundred sixty-three (3663), thirty-six hundred sixty-four (3664), thirty-six hundred sixty-five (3665), thirty-six hundred sixty-nine (3669), thirty-six hundred seventy (3670), thirty-six hundred seventy-two (3672), thirty-six hundred seventy-three (3673), thirty-six hundred seventy-four (3674), thirty-six hundred seventy-five (3675), and thirty-six hundred eighty-four (3684) of the code, 1924, be and the same are hereby repealed.

Approved March 28, A. D. 1925.

CHAPTER 81

PATERNITY

S. F. 134

AN ACT to repeal sections twelve thousand six hundred fifty-eight (12658) to twelve thousand six hundred sixty-seven (12667), both inclusive, code, 1924, relating to children born out of wedlock and to enact a substitute therefor, being an act with reference to proceedings to establish paternity.

Be it enacted by the General Assembly of the State of Iowa:

SECTION 1. **Obligation of parents.** The parents of a child born out of wedlock and not legitimized (in this act referred to as "the child") owe the child necessary maintenance, education and support. They are also liable for the child's funeral expenses. The father is also liable to pay the expense of the mother's pregnancy and confinement. The obligation of the parent to support the child under the laws for the support of poor relatives applies to children born out of wedlock.

SEC. 2. **Recovery by mother from father.** The mother may recover from the father a reasonable share of the necessary support of the child. In the absence of a previous demand in writing (served personally or by registered letter addressed to the father at his last known residence or in the manner provided for service of original notices) not more than two years' support furnished prior to the bringing of the action may be recovered.

SEC. 3. **Recovery by others than mother.** The obligation of the father as hereby provided creates also a cause of action on behalf of the legal representative of the mother, or on behalf of third persons furnishing support or defraying the reasonable expenses thereof, where paternity has been judicially established by proceedings brought by the mother or by or on behalf of the child or by the authorities charged with its support, or where paternity has been acknowledged by the father in writing or by the part performance of the obligations imposed upon him.

SEC. 4. **Discharge of father's obligation.** The obligation of the

Figure 22: *Acts*, ch.81 (Iowa, 1925)

Kansas

Kansas was the last state to reference prenatal child support from the father, doing so in 2006. Yet, it is unique in how the legislature worded the laws, writing them in the negative with the presumption that the father *did* provide support (for the the second trimester onward). After searching through a century of statute annotations, I found no references to precedent set in Kansas courts. Yet, it is possible that the state had judicial precedent influenced by its neighbors, Colorado and Nebraska, which both had prenatal child support established by judicial precedent decades before their legislatures enacted it.

Sixteen years before the legislature added a prenatal child support reference to Chapter 38 (*Minors*), they added references to Title 59 (*Probate Court*) concerning adoptions. Though the statutes contain several additional references to coverage of prenatal expenses by the adoptive parents, I have only included those that also reference the biological father to stay within scope.

Kansas Statutes Annotated, §38-2271(a) *(Presumption of unfitness; HB 2352, 2006)*
(10) a father, after having knowledge of the pregnancy, failed without reasonable cause to **provide support for the mother during the six months prior to the child's birth**;
(11) a father abandoned the mother after having knowledge of the pregnancy

Kansas Statutes Annotated, §59-2136(e) *(Relinquishment and adoption; SB 431, 1990 sec 25; amended in HB 2665, 2006)*
Except as provided in subsection (d), if a mother desires to relinquish or consents to the adoption of such mother's child, a petition shall be filed in the district court to terminate the parental rights of the father, unless the father's relationship to the child has been previously terminated or determined not to exist by a court. The petition may be filed by the mother, the petitioner for adoption, the person or agency having custody of the child or the agency to which the child has been or is to be relinquished. Where appropriate, the request to terminate parental rights may be contained in a petition for adoption. If the request to terminate parental rights is not filed in connection with an adoption proceeding, venue shall be in the county in which the child, the mother or the presumed or alleged father resides or is found. In an effort to identify the father, the court shall determine by deposition, affidavit or hearing, the following:
...
(5) **whether the mother has received support payments or promises of support with respect to the child or in connection with such mother's pregnancy**; and
...

Figure 23: HB 2352 (Kansas, 2006)

Kansas Statutes Annotated, §59-2136(h)(1) *(Relinquishment and adoption; SB 431, 1990; amended in HB 2665, 2006)*
(D) a father, after having knowledge of the pregnancy, failed without reasonable cause to **provide support for the mother during the six months prior to the child's birth**;
(E) a father abandoned the mother after having knowledge of the pregnancy

Kentucky

In 1923, the *Kentucky Children's Code Commission* issued a report[24] concerning the state of child welfare legislation through 1922. Among many topics, the *Commission* addressed illegitimacy. Within their recommendation was that mothers and children would benefit from requiring the fathers to pay "expenses of prosecution and the reasonable expenses of the mother during confinement and for a period of eight weeks thereafter." It wasn't until 1964 that these recommendations became law.

Kentucky Revised Statutes, §406.011 *(Uniform Act on Paternity, Obligations of the father; Acts 1964, ch.37, §1)*
The father of a child which is or may be born out of wedlock is liable to the same extent as the father of a child born in wedlock, whether or not the child is born alive, for the **reasonable expense of the mother's pregnancy and confinement** and for the education, necessary support and funeral expenses of the child. A child born during lawful wedlock, or within ten (10) months thereafter, is presumed to be the child of the husband and wife. However, a child born out of wedlock includes a child born to a married woman by a man other than her husband where evidence shows that the marital relationship between the husband and wife ceased ten (10) months prior to the birth of the child.

Figure 24: *Acts*, ch.37 (Ky., 1964)

Kentucky Revised Statutes, §406.021(3) *(Liability of noncustodial parent; Acts 1964 ch.37 §2)*
If paternity has been determined or has been acknowledged according to the laws of this state, the liabilities of the noncustodial parent may be enforced in the same or other proceedings by the mother, child, person, or agency substantially **contributing to the cost of pregnancy, confinement**, education, necessary support, or funeral expenses. Bills for testing, **pregnancy, and childbirth** without requiring third party foundation testimony shall be regarded as prima facie evidence of the amount incurred. An action to enforce the liabilities of the noncustodial parent shall be brought by the county attorney upon the request of such complainant authorized by this section. An action to enforce the liabilities of the cost of pregnancy, birthing costs, child support, and medical support shall be brought by the county attorney or by the Cabinet for Health and Family Services or its designee.

Figure 25: Kentucky Children's Code Commission

Louisiana

As of 1933, Louisiana — along with Alaska, Texas, Virginia, and Puerto Rico — had no formal Civil Code in place for acknowledgement of paternity.[25] In the 1960s and 1970s, Louisiana adopted several Uniform laws relating to reciprocity of support orders within other US states, but prenatal child support was absent in each instance, finally being added in 1995.

Children's Code, 1302:1(A) *(Basis for jurisdiction over nonresident; Acts 1995, No. 251, HB1518)*

In a proceeding to establish or enforce a support order or to determine parentage of a child, a tribunal of this state may exercise personal jurisdiction over a nonresident individual or the individual's guardian, curator, or tutor, if: ... (4) The individual resided in this state and provided **prenatal expenses** or support for the child;

Children's Code, 1303:16(D) *(Special rules of evidence and procedure; Acts 1995 No. 251, HB1518)*

Copies of bills for testing for parentage and for **prenatal and postnatal health care of the mother and child**, furnished to the adverse party at least ten days before trial, are admissible in evidence to prove the amount of the charges billed and that the charges were reasonable, necessary, and customary.

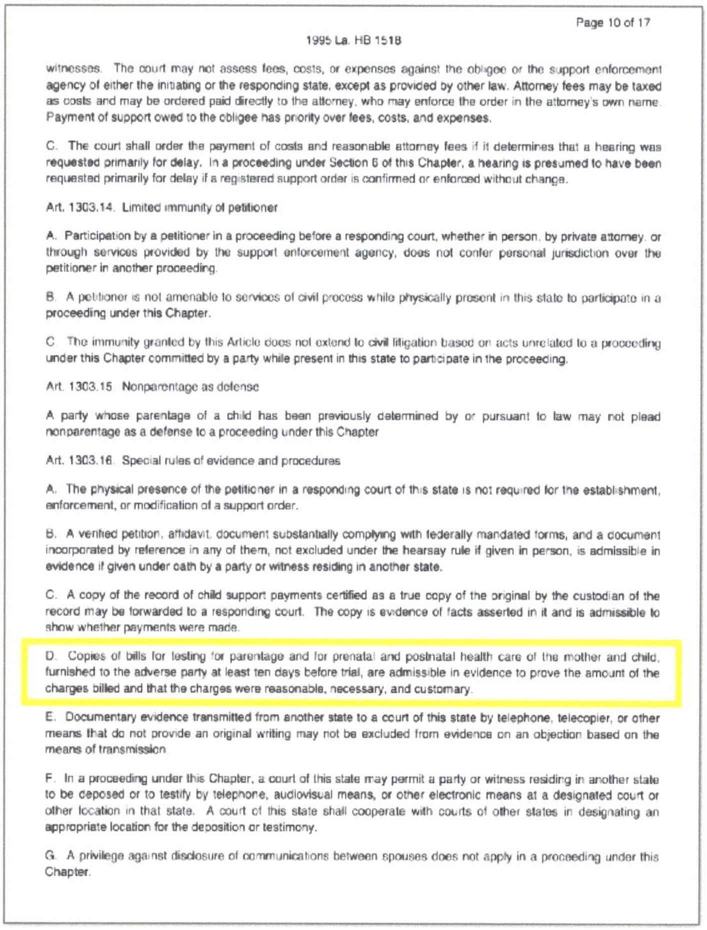

Page 10 of 17

1995 La. HB 1518

witnesses. The court may not assess fees, costs, or expenses against the obligee or the support enforcement agency of either the initiating or the responding state, except as provided by other law. Attorney fees may be taxed as costs and may be ordered paid directly to the attorney, who may enforce the order in the attorney's own name. Payment of support owed to the obligee has priority over fees, costs, and expenses.

C. The court shall order the payment of costs and reasonable attorney fees if it determines that a hearing was requested primarily for delay. In a proceeding under Section 6 of this Chapter, a hearing is presumed to have been requested primarily for delay if a registered support order is confirmed or enforced without change.

Art. 1303.14. Limited immunity of petitioner

A. Participation by a petitioner in a proceeding before a responding court, whether in person, by private attorney, or through services provided by the support enforcement agency, does not confer personal jurisdiction over the petitioner in another proceeding.

B. A petitioner is not amenable to services of civil process while physically present in this state to participate in a proceeding under this Chapter.

C. The immunity granted by this Article does not extend to civil litigation based on acts unrelated to a proceeding under this Chapter committed by a party while present in this state to participate in the proceeding.

Art. 1303.15. Nonparentage as defense

A party whose parentage of a child has been previously determined by or pursuant to law may not plead nonparentage as a defense to a proceeding under this Chapter

Art. 1303.16. Special rules of evidence and procedures

A. The physical presence of the petitioner in a responding court of this state is not required for the establishment, enforcement, or modification of a support order.

B. A verified petition, affidavit, document substantially complying with federally mandated forms, and a document incorporated by reference in any of them, not excluded under the hearsay rule if given in person, is admissible in evidence if given under oath by a party or witness residing in another state.

C. A copy of the record of child support payments certified as a true copy of the original by the custodian of the record may be forwarded to a responding court. The copy is evidence of facts asserted in it and is admissible to show whether payments were made.

D. Copies of bills for testing for parentage and for prenatal and postnatal health care of the mother and child, furnished to the adverse party at least ten days before trial, are admissible in evidence to prove the amount of the charges billed and that the charges were reasonable, necessary, and customary.

E. Documentary evidence transmitted from another state to a court of this state by telephone, telecopier, or other means that do not provide an original writing may not be excluded from evidence on an objection based on the means of transmission.

F. In a proceeding under this Chapter, a court of this state may permit a party or witness residing in another state to be deposed or to testify by telephone, audiovisual means, or other electronic means at a designated court or other location in that state. A court of this state shall cooperate with courts of other states in designating an appropriate location for the deposition or testimony.

G. A privilege against disclosure of communications between spouses does not apply in a proceeding under this Chapter.

Figure 26: *Acts*, No. 251 (La., 1995)

Maine

Revised Statutes of 1916, c.102 §7 *(Judgments in Bastardy Cases; Public Laws 1909, c.111 to amend Revised Statutes of 1903, c.99, §7)*

If, on such issue, the jury finds the respondent If respondent not guilty, he shall be discharged; but if they find him guilty, or the facts in the declaration filed are admitted by default or on demurrer, he shall be adjudged the father of such child; stand charged with its maintenance, with the assistance of the mother, as the court orders; and shall be ordered to pay the complainant her costs of suit and for **the expense of her delivery, and of her nursing, medicine and medical attendance, during the period of her sickness and convalescence**, and of the support of such child to the date of rendition of judgment; and shall give a bond, with sufficient sureties approved by the court, to the complainant to perform said order, and a bond, with sufficient sureties so approved, to the town liable for the maintenance of such child, and be committed until he gives them. The latter bond shall be deposited with the clerk of the court for the use of such town. If the respondent does not comply with that part of the order relative to payment of expenses and costs of suit, execution may issue therefor as in actions of tort.

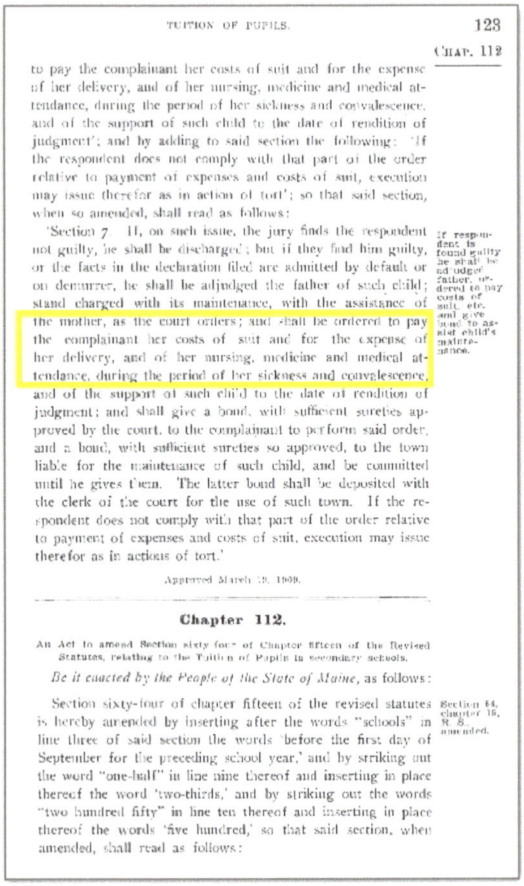
TUITION OF PUPILS. 123

CHAP. 112

to pay the complainant her costs of suit and for the expense of her delivery, and of her nursing, medicine and medical attendance, during the period of her sickness and convalescence, and of the support of such child to the date of rendition of judgment'; and by adding to said section the following: 'If the respondent does not comply with that part of the order relative to payment of expenses and costs of suit, execution may issue therefor as in action of tort'; so that said section, when so amended, shall read as follows:

'Section 7. If, on such issue, the jury finds the respondent not guilty, he shall be discharged; but if they find him guilty, or the facts in the declaration filed are admitted by default or on demurrer, he shall be adjudged the father of such child; stand charged with its maintenance, with the assistance of the mother, as the court orders; and shall be ordered to pay the complainant her costs of suit and for the expense of her delivery, and of her nursing, medicine and medical attendance, during the period of her sickness and convalescence, and of the support of such child to the date of rendition of judgment; and shall give a bond, with sufficient sureties approved by the court, to the complainant to perform said order, and a bond, with sufficient sureties so approved, to the town liable for the maintenance of such child, and be committed until he gives them. The latter bond shall be deposited with the clerk of the court for the use of such town. If the respondent does not comply with that part of the order relative to payment of expenses and costs of suit, execution may issue therefor as in actions of tort.'

If respondent is found guilty he shall be adjudged father, ordered to pay costs of suit, etc. and give bond to assist child's maintenance.

Approved March 19, 1909.

Chapter 112.

An Act to amend Section sixty-four of Chapter fifteen of the Revised Statutes, relating to the Tuition of Pupils in secondary schools.

Be it enacted by the People of the State of Maine, as follows:

Section sixty-four of chapter fifteen of the revised statutes is hereby amended by inserting after the words "schools" in line three of said section the words 'before the first day of September for the preceding school year,' and by striking out the word "one-half" in line nine thereof and inserting in place thereof the word 'two-thirds,' and by striking out the words "two hundred fifty" in line ten thereof and inserting in place thereof the words 'five hundred,' so that said section, when amended, shall read as follows:

Section 64, chapter 15, R. S., amended.

Figure 27: *Public Laws*, c.111 (Maine, 1909)

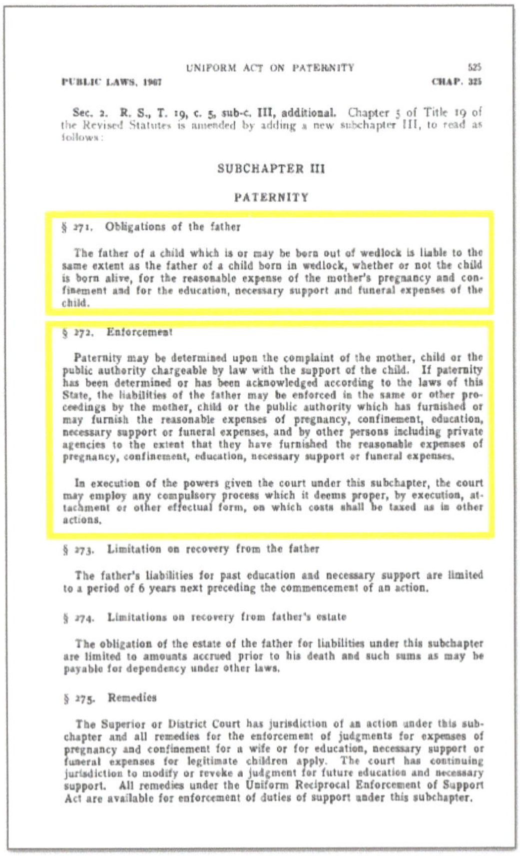
UNIFORM ACT ON PATERNITY 525

PUBLIC LAWS, 1967 CHAP. 325

Sec. 2. R. S., T. 19, c. 5, sub-c. III, additional. Chapter 5 of Title 19 of the Revised Statutes is amended by adding a new subchapter III, to read as follows:

SUBCHAPTER III

PATERNITY

§ 271. Obligations of the father

The father of a child which is or may be born out of wedlock is liable to the same extent as the father of a child born in wedlock, whether or not the child is born alive, for the reasonable expense of the mother's pregnancy and confinement and for the education, necessary support and funeral expenses of the child.

§ 272. Enforcement

Paternity may be determined upon the complaint of the mother, child or the public authority chargeable by law with the support of the child. If paternity has been determined or has been acknowledged according to the laws of this State, the liabilities of the father may be enforced in the same or other proceedings by the mother, child or the public authority which has furnished or may furnish the reasonable expenses of pregnancy, confinement, education, necessary support or funeral expenses, and by other persons including private agencies to the extent that they have furnished the reasonable expenses of pregnancy, confinement, education, necessary support or funeral expenses.

In execution of the powers given the court under this subchapter, the court may employ any compulsory process which it deems proper, by execution, attachment or other effectual form, on which costs shall be taxed as in other actions.

§ 273. Limitation on recovery from the father

The father's liabilities for past education and necessary support are limited to a period of 6 years next preceding the commencement of an action.

§ 274. Limitations on recovery from father's estate

The obligation of the estate of the father for liabilities under this subchapter are limited to amounts accrued prior to his death and such sums as may be payable for dependency under other laws.

§ 275. Remedies

The Superior or District Court has jurisdiction of an action under this subchapter and all remedies for the enforcement of judgments for expenses of pregnancy and confinement for a wife or for education, necessary support or funeral expenses for legitimate children apply. The court has continuing jurisdiction to modify or revoke a judgment for future education and necessary support. All remedies under the Uniform Reciprocal Enforcement of Support Act are available for enforcement of duties of support under this subchapter.

Figure 28: *Public Laws*, c.325 (Maine, 1967)

Revised Statutes of 1964,
Title 19-A, §1552 *(Uniform Act on Paternity; Public Laws 1967, c.325 as 19 MRSA §271)*

The father of a child is liable for the **reasonable expense of the mother's pregnancy and confinement** and for the education, support and funeral expenses of the child.

Revised Statutes of 1964, Title 19-A, §1553 *(Uniform Act on Paternity; Public Laws 1967, c.325 as 19 MRSA §272)*

If paternity has been determined or has been acknowledged according to the laws of this State, the liabilities of the father may be enforced in the same or other proceedings by the mother, the child or the public authority that has furnished or may furnish the **reasonable expenses of pregnancy, confinement**, education, support or funeral expenses, and by other persons, including private agencies, to the extent that they have furnished the **reasonable expenses of pregnancy, confinement**, education, support or funeral expenses. Bills and records of **expenses paid for pregnancy, childbirth** and genetic testing are admissible as evidence without requiring 3rd-party foundation testimony and are prima facie evidence of amounts incurred for those services or for testing on behalf of the child. Chapter 63 applies to an award of past support, which is calculated by applying the current child support guidelines to the period for which past support is owed

Maryland

Maryland's earliest reference to prenatal child support came in *William Holmes v. Walter Mitchell, et al.*[26], an 1850 lawsuit that aimed to resolve a dispute relating to annual proceeds from the farm Ignatius Semmes left in his will to his aunt and uncle. This farm had an unspecified number of slaves, and the issue arose of how the trustee of the estate should handle pregnancies of the women. The opinion of the Court was that the trustee is responsible for paying from the estate's income the expenses for infancy and "to take care of the parent during her pregnancy." This case, however, was of very narrow scope, so it cannot be taken as a blanket requirement for prenatal child support.

Maryland Annotated Code, Art. 12 § 5 *(Bastardy and Fornication; Laws 1920, ch. 564)*
...and **further to pay the whole or such part of the expenses incurred by the said mother during her confinement** as the court may direct and to pay the reasonable funeral expenses of said child if he or she shall die under the age of twelve years;

Maryland Annotated Code of 1957, Art. 16 § 66H(a) *(Chancery, Paternity Proceedings; Acts 1963 ch.722)*
In addition to providing for the support and maintenance of the child, the order also may require the defendant to pay all or any part of the **mother's medical and hospital expense for her pregnancy, confinement, and recovery**, and for the funeral expenses if the child has died or dies; and in addition thereto, may award counsel fees to the attorney representing the complainant or petitioner. Costs shall be awarded as in other civil cases in accordance with Rule 604 of the Maryland Rules of Practice and Procedure; provided, that the Court, in its discretion, may order that all or any part of the costs shall be paid by the county or City of Baltimore, as the case may be, where the proceedings were instituted.

Figure 29: *Laws*, ch.564 (Md., 1920)

Maryland Code, §5-1033(A) *(Retroactive child support; Acts 1984 ch.296 p.2051, 2052)*
In general
(a) In a paternity proceeding, the court may order the father or the mother to pay all or part of any 1 or more of the following:
(1) the support of the child;
(2) the **mother's medical and hospital expenses for pregnancy, childbirth, and recovery**; and
(3) the funeral expenses of the child.
Records admissible as evidence
(b) Subject to the right of any party to subpoena a custodian of records at least 10 days before trial, any records relating to the **cost of the mother's medical and hospital expenses for pregnancy, childbirth, and recovery and any neonatal expenses of the child** shall be admissible in evidence without the presence of a custodian of records and shall constitute prima facie evidence of the amount of expenses incurred.
Orders against father
(c) The court in a paternity proceeding may order the father to pay either or both of the following:
(1) all or part of the medical support of the child, **including neonatal expenses**; and
(2) counsel fees to the counsel who represents the complainant.

Maryland Code, §12-101(d) *(Retroactive child support; Acts 1994, ch.113)*
(1) The court may order either parent to pay all or part of:
(i) the **mother's medical and hospital expenses for pregnancy, confinement, and recovery**; and
(ii) medical support for the child, **including neonatal expenses**.

Figure 30: *Acts*, ch.722 (Md., 1963)

Massachusetts

Uncodified Act *(Illegitimate children and their maintenance; Act 1913, ch.563)*
Section 4. If the child has not been born at the time of such adjudication, the court or justice having jurisdiction of the case shall continue the case from time to time until the child is born. At any time after such adjudication, after inquiring into the respective means of the defendant and the mother, the court or justice having jurisdiction of the case may make an order for the payment to the mother or to a probation officer of a sum of money to be determined by the court or justice for the **expenses of the confinement of the mother**, and for failure to comply with such order may order that the defendant be committed to jail, as for a contempt of court, for a term not exceeding two months, unless he shall sooner comply with the order of the court.
Section 5. After such adjudication, the court or justice having jurisdiction of the case may make such order as may be considered expedient relative to the care and custody of the child, and afterward from time to time may revise and alter the said order, as justice and the welfare of the child require, and the order shall be binding on all persons.

Massachusetts General Laws, Ch 273, §13 *(Desertion, non-support, and illegitimacy; Act 1977, ch.848, sec.5, repealed in Acts 1986, ch.310, sec.25)*
~~No law limiting adjournments or continuances shall apply to any proceedings under sections twelve to eighteen, inclusive. If the child has not been born at the time of the adjudication, the court shall continue the case from time to time until the child is born. At any time after adjudication, after inquiring into the respective means of the alleged father and the mother, the court having jurisdiction of the case may make an order for the payment to the mother or to a probation officer of a sum of money determined by the court for the **expenses of the pregnancy and of the confinement of the mother**, whether the child is born dead or alive. If the child has died, or subsequently if the child dies, the court may make an order for the payment of its funeral expenses, whether or not other relief is sought. For failure to comply with any such order the court may order the alleged father committed to jail, as for a contempt of court, for a term not exceeding two months, unless he shall sooner comply therewith.~~

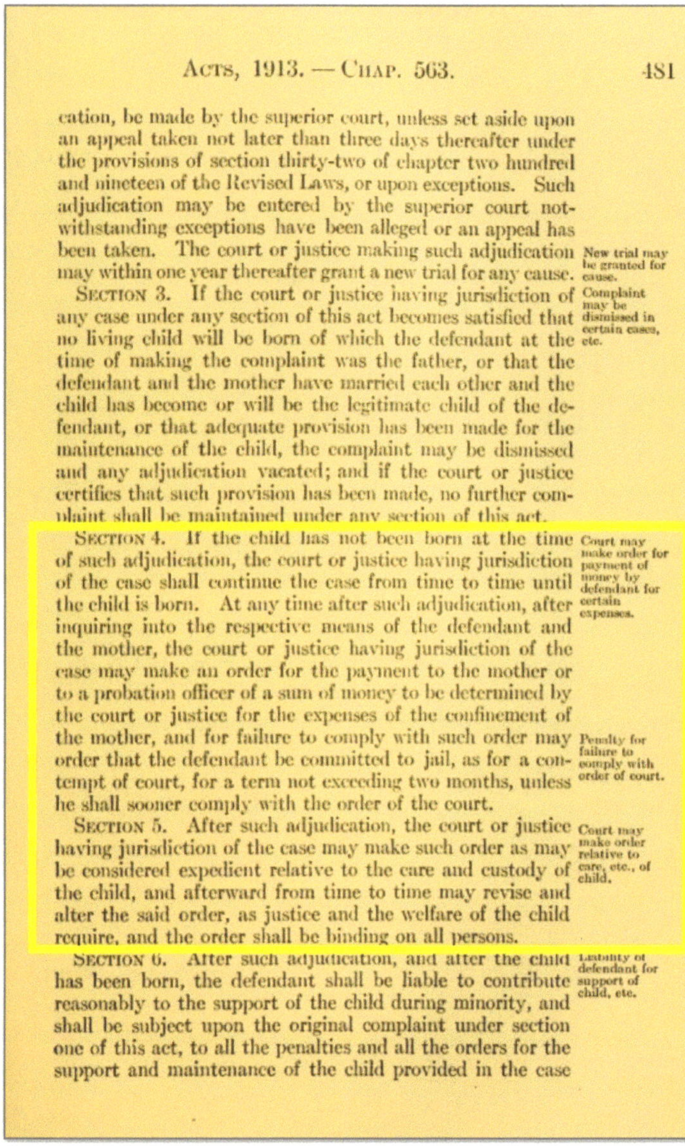
ACTS, 1913. — CHAP. 563. 481

cation, be made by the superior court, unless set aside upon an appeal taken not later than three days thereafter under the provisions of section thirty-two of chapter two hundred and nineteen of the Revised Laws, or upon exceptions. Such adjudication may be entered by the superior court notwithstanding exceptions have been alleged or an appeal has been taken. The court or justice making such adjudication may within one year thereafter grant a new trial for any cause.

New trial may be granted for cause.

SECTION 3. If the court or justice having jurisdiction of any case under any section of this act becomes satisfied that no living child will be born of which the defendant at the time of making the complaint was the father, or that the defendant and the mother have married each other and the child has become or will be the legitimate child of the defendant, or that adequate provision has been made for the maintenance of the child, the complaint may be dismissed and any adjudication vacated; and if the court or justice certifies that such provision has been made, no further complaint shall be maintained under any section of this act.

Complaint may be dismissed in certain cases, etc.

SECTION 4. If the child has not been born at the time of such adjudication, the court or justice having jurisdiction of the case shall continue the case from time to time until the child is born. At any time after such adjudication, after inquiring into the respective means of the defendant and the mother, the court or justice having jurisdiction of the case may make an order for the payment to the mother or to a probation officer of a sum of money to be determined by the court or justice for the expenses of the confinement of the mother, and for failure to comply with such order may order that the defendant be committed to jail, as for a contempt of court, for a term not exceeding two months, unless he shall sooner comply with the order of the court.

Court may make order for payment of money by defendant for certain expenses.

Penalty for failure to comply with order of court.

SECTION 5. After such adjudication, the court or justice having jurisdiction of the case may make such order as may be considered expedient relative to the care and custody of the child, and afterward from time to time may revise and alter the said order, as justice and the welfare of the child require, and the order shall be binding on all persons.

Court may make order relative to care, etc., of child.

SECTION 6. After such adjudication, and after the child has been born, the defendant shall be liable to contribute reasonably to the support of the child during minority, and shall be subject upon the original complaint under section one of this act, to all the penalties and all the orders for the support and maintenance of the child provided in the case

Liability of defendant for support of child, etc.

Figure 31: *Acts*, ch.563 (Mass., 1913)

Massachusetts General Laws, Ch 209C, §9(a) *(Judgment or order for support; Session Laws 1993, ch.460, sec.73, approved in 1994)*
...An order may be entered requiring a parent chargeable with support to reimburse the mother or the department of transitional assistance or the office of Medicaid or the executive office of health and human services for medical expenses attributable to the child or **associated with childbirth or resulting from the pregnancy**.

Michigan

Until about the year 2000, all Michigan legislation and court cases included two sets of numbering: one for the *Michigan Compiled Laws* and one for the now-deprecated *Michigan Statutes Annotated*. The laws were identical under both numbering systems. *The Paternity Act* includes the MSA reference in brackets.

Michigan Compiled Laws, §722.712(1) *(The Paternity Act; Act 205 sec 2(1), 1956)*
The parents of a child born out of wedlock are liable for all of the following:
(a) The medical expenses connected to the mother's pregnancy.
(b) The medical expenses connected to the birth of the child.
(c) The necessary support and education of the child.
(d) The child's funeral expenses.

Michigan Compiled Laws, §722.1498(2) *(Duty to pay child support; Act 366 sec 8(2), 2014)*
The parents of a child born out of wedlock are also liable for the **medical expenses connected to the mother's pregnancy and the child's birth** to the same extent and in the same manner as those expenses are allowed under the paternity act, 1956 PA 205, MCL 722.711 to 722.730.

408 PUBLIC ACTS 1956—No. 205.

259.555 Same; advancement of funds.
Sec. 5. Provisions of this act shall be construed to authorize advancement of funds with respect to all items of airport development on publicly owned airports and landing fields, except that no such funds shall be used for the acquisition of land.

259.556 Same; allocation of unencumbered funds.
Sec. 6. If any unit of local government on an approved program shall fail to notify the Michigan department of aeronautics within 60 days of the effective date of this act, that said unit of local government desires to participate in matching funds for airport construction and improvement, the state administrative board, on the recommendation of the controller of the department of administration, may allocate all or any part of the unencumbered funds among the other units of local government, such allocation to be on the basis of the greatest need for airport facilities as determined by the Michigan aeronautics commission.

259.557 Construction of act.
Sec. 7. This act shall be construed as supplemental to the laws of this state relative to improvement of airports.
This act is ordered to take immediate effect.
Approved April 26, 1956.

[No. 205.]

AN ACT to confer upon circuit courts jurisdiction over proceedings to compel and provide support of children born out of wedlock; to prescribe the procedure for determination of such liability; to authorize agreements providing for furnishing of such support and to provide for the enforcement thereof; and to prescribe penalties for the violation of certain provisions of this act.

The People of the State of Michigan enact:

722.711 Paternity act; definitions. [M.S.A. 25.491]
Sec. 1. (a) A child born out of wedlock is a child begotten and born to any woman who was unmarried from the conception to the date of birth of the child.
(b) When the word "child" is used in this act it shall refer to a child so born out of wedlock.
(c) When the word "mother" is used in this act it shall refer to the mother of a child so born out of wedlock.
(d) When the word "court" is used in this act it shall refer to the circuit court.

722.712 Child born out of wedlock; liability of parents. [M.S.A. 25.492]
Sec. 2. (a) The parents of a child so born out of wedlock are liable for the necessary support and education of the child. They are also liable for the child's funeral expenses. The father is liable to pay the expenses of the mother's confinement, and is also liable to pay such expenses in connection with her pregnancy as the court in its discretion may deem proper.
(b) If the father dies, an order of filiation or a judicially approved settlement made prior to his death shall be enforceable against his estate in the same manner and way as a divorce decree.

722.713 Father's agreement for support and education. [M.S.A. 25.493]
Sec. 3. (a) An agreement or compromise made by the mother or child or by some authorized person on their behalf with the father concerning the support and education of the child shall be binding upon the mother and the child only when the court having jurisdiction to compel support and education of the child shall have determined that adequate provision is reasonably secured by payment or otherwise and has approved the agreement or compromise.

Figure 32: Act 205 (Mich., 1956)

Minnesota

Minnesota is unique in that the father has been expected to assist with "the mother's lost wages due to medical necessity" since 1980.

General Statutes, 1913, §17.3219 *(Father to pay all expenses; SL 1921 ch. 489)*
In the event of judgment of paternity as provided in section 3218 the mother shall be entitled to recover of the father in a civil action **all expense necessarily incurred by her in connection with her confinement, including her suitable maintenance for not more than eight weeks next prior thereto** and not more than eight weeks thereafter; and for the burial of the child if the same shall have been still born, or shall have died after birth, **and all necessary expenses and doctor's bills in connection with her or said child's sickness**. The provisions of this section shall apply only to such expense or portion thereof as is not otherwise provided for by order of the court.

Minnesota Statutes, §257.66(3) *(Recognition of parentage; Session Laws 1980, c.589)*
The judgment or order shall contain provisions concerning the duty of support, the custody of the child, the name of the child, the Social Security number of the mother, father, and child, if known at the time of adjudication, parenting time with the child, the furnishing of bond or other security for the payment of the judgment, or any other matter in the best interest of the child. Custody and parenting time and all subsequent motions related to them shall proceed and be determined under section 257.541. The remaining matters and all subsequent motions related to them shall proceed and be determined in accordance with chapters 518 and 518A. The judgment or order may direct the appropriate party to pay all or a proportion of the **reasonable expenses of the mother's pregnancy and confinement, including the mother's lost wages due to medical necessity**, after consideration of the relevant facts, including the relative financial means of the parents; the earning ability of each parent; and any health insurance policies held by either parent, or by a spouse or parent of the parent, which would provide benefits for the **expenses incurred by the mother during her pregnancy and confinement**. Pregnancy and confinement expenses and genetic testing costs, submitted by the public authority, are admissible as evidence without third-party foundation testimony and constitute prima facie evidence of the amounts incurred for those services or for the genetic testing. Remedies available for the collection and enforcement of child support apply to confinement costs and are considered additional child support.

Minnesota Statutes, §257.75(3)(v) *(Recognition of parentage; Session Laws 1993Sp, c.1)*
ordering a contribution to the **reasonable expenses of the mother's pregnancy and confinement**, as provided under section 257.66, subdivision 3

Minnesota Statutes, §518A.60(a) *(Session Laws 1997, c.245)*
Remedies available for the collection and enforcement of support in this chapter and chapters 256, 257, 518, and 518C also apply to cases in which the child or children for whom support is owed are emancipated and the obligor owes past support or has an accumulated arrearage as of the date of the youngest child's emancipation. Child support arrearages under this section include arrearages for child support, medical support, child care, **pregnancy and birth expenses**, and unreimbursed medical expenses as defined in section 518A.41, subdivision 1, paragraph (h).

Figure 33: *Laws*, ch.489 (Minn., 1921)

Figure 34: *Laws*, ch.589 (Minn., 1980)

Mississippi

Mississippi was the first of at least four states to enact the *Uniform Law on Paternity*, doing so in 1962. This particular legislation had many similarities to the 1973 *Uniform Parentage Act* that all states eventually enacted in some form (though not necessarily the prenatal child support component).

Mississippi Code Annotated, §93-9-7 *(Uniform Law on Paternity, Obligations of father, Session Laws 1962, ch.312 §1, HB230)*
The father of a child which is or may be born out of lawful matrimony is liable to the same extent as the father of a child born of lawful matrimony, whether or not the child is born alive, for the **reasonable expense of the mother's pregnancy and confinement**, and for the education, necessary support and maintenance, and medical and funeral expenses of the child. A child born out of lawful matrimony also includes a child born to a married woman by a man other than her lawful husband.

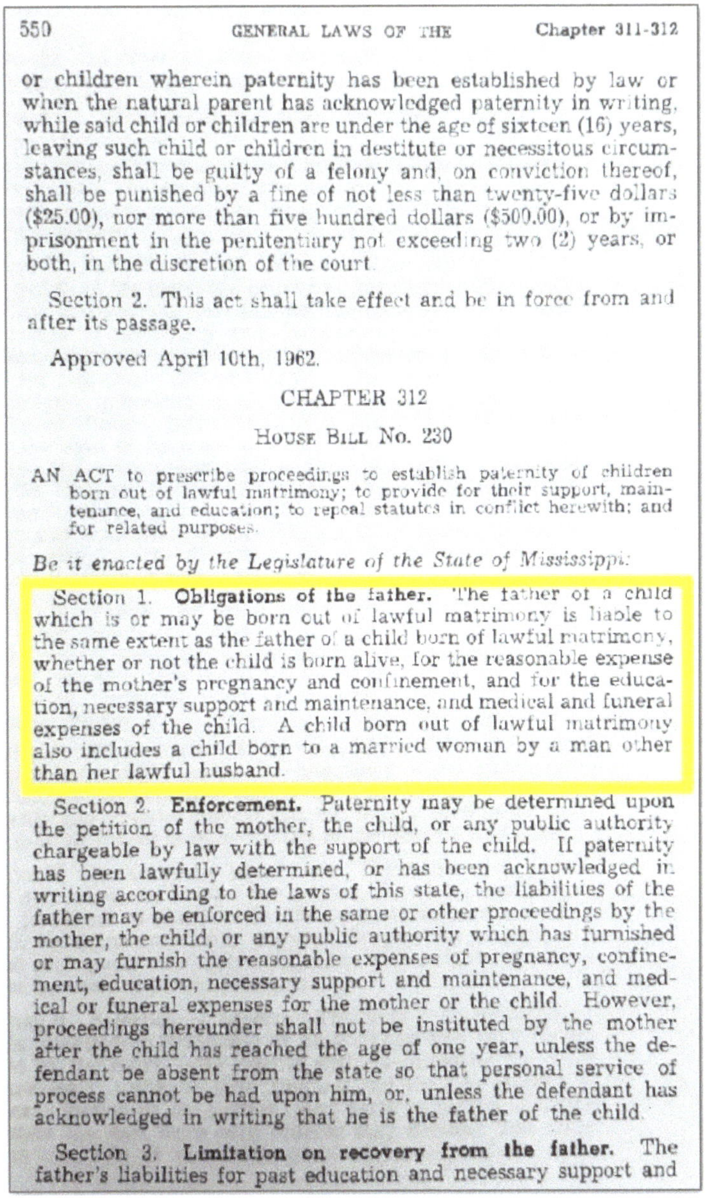

550 GENERAL LAWS OF THE Chapter 311-312

or children wherein paternity has been established by law or when the natural parent has acknowledged paternity in writing, while said child or children are under the age of sixteen (16) years, leaving such child or children in destitute or necessitous circumstances, shall be guilty of a felony and, on conviction thereof, shall be punished by a fine of not less than twenty-five dollars ($25.00), nor more than five hundred dollars ($500.00), or by imprisonment in the penitentiary not exceeding two (2) years, or both, in the discretion of the court.

Section 2. This act shall take effect and be in force from and after its passage.

Approved April 10th, 1962.

CHAPTER 312

HOUSE BILL No. 230

AN ACT to prescribe proceedings to establish paternity of children born out of lawful matrimony; to provide for their support, maintenance, and education; to repeal statutes in conflict herewith; and for related purposes.

Be it enacted by the Legislature of the State of Mississippi:

Section 1. **Obligations of the father.** The father of a child which is or may be born out of lawful matrimony is liable to the same extent as the father of a child born of lawful matrimony, whether or not the child is born alive, for the reasonable expense of the mother's pregnancy and confinement, and for the education, necessary support and maintenance, and medical and funeral expenses of the child. A child born out of lawful matrimony also includes a child born to a married woman by a man other than her lawful husband.

Section 2. **Enforcement.** Paternity may be determined upon the petition of the mother, the child, or any public authority chargeable by law with the support of the child. If paternity has been lawfully determined, or has been acknowledged in writing according to the laws of this state, the liabilities of the father may be enforced in the same or other proceedings by the mother, the child, or any public authority which has furnished or may furnish the reasonable expenses of pregnancy, confinement, education, necessary support and maintenance, and medical or funeral expenses for the mother or the child. However, proceedings hereunder shall not be instituted by the mother after the child has reached the age of one year, unless the defendant be absent from the state so that personal service of process cannot be had upon him, or, unless the defendant has acknowledged in writing that he is the father of the child.

Section 3. **Limitation on recovery from the father.** The father's liabilities for past education and necessary support and

Figure 35: *Session Laws*, ch.312 (Miss., 1962)

Missouri

In 1986, the *Missouri General Assembly* passed *HB 1596*[27], which enacted *Missouri Revised Statutes* § 1.205[28], making the value statement, in subsection 2, that "[e]ffective January 1, 1988, the laws of this state shall be interpreted and construed to acknowledge on behalf of the unborn child at every stage of development, all the rights, privileges, and immunities available to other persons, citizens, and residents of this state…" Concerning prenatal child support, the *General Assembly* made good on their intent and passed the first such requirements on July 15, 1987, thereby going into effect by the close of that year.

Missouri Revised Statutes § 210.839(6) *(Judgment or order,; 1997 SB 361)*

Copies of any **paid or unpaid bill for pregnancy, childbirth** or genetic testing shall be admitted as evidence without requiring third-party foundation testimony if such copies have been provided to all parties not less than seven days prior to trial. Such copies shall constitute prima facie evidence of the amounts incurred for such services or testing.

Missouri Revised Statutes § 210.841(3) *(Judgment or order,; 1987 SB 328 sec.15 p.652)*

The judgment or order shall contain the Social Security number of each party and may contain any other provision directed against the appropriate party to the proceeding concerning: ... (5) Any matter in the best interest of the child. The judgment or order may direct the father to pay the **reasonable expenses of the mother's pregnancy and confinement**.

Missouri Revised Statutes § 210.843(1) *(Judgment or order,; 1987 SB 328 sec.17 p.652)*

The judgment or order shall contain the Social Security number of each party and may contain any other provision directed against the appropriate party to the proceeding concerning: ... (5) Any matter in the best interest of the child. The judgment or order may direct the father to pay the **reasonable expenses of the mother's pregnancy and confinement**.

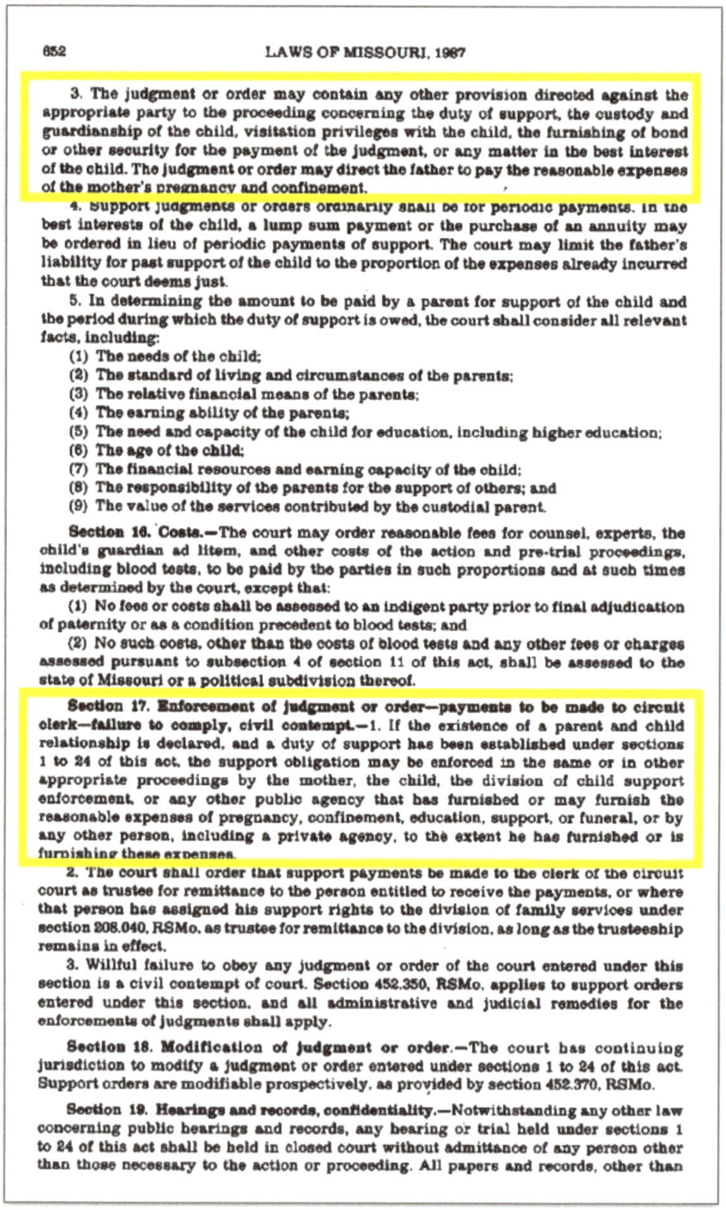

652 LAWS OF MISSOURI, 1987

3. The judgment or order may contain any other provision directed against the appropriate party to the proceeding concerning the duty of support, the custody and guardianship of the child, visitation privileges with the child, the furnishing of bond or other security for the payment of the judgment, or any matter in the best interest of the child. The judgment or order may direct the father to pay the reasonable expenses of the mother's pregnancy and confinement.

4. Support judgments or orders ordinarily shall be for periodic payments. In the best interests of the child, a lump sum payment or the purchase of an annuity may be ordered in lieu of periodic payments of support. The court may limit the father's liability for past support of the child to the proportion of the expenses already incurred that the court deems just.

5. In determining the amount to be paid by a parent for support of the child and the period during which the duty of support is owed, the court shall consider all relevant facts, including:

(1) The needs of the child;
(2) The standard of living and circumstances of the parents;
(3) The relative financial means of the parents;
(4) The earning ability of the parents;
(5) The need and capacity of the child for education, including higher education;
(6) The age of the child;
(7) The financial resources and earning capacity of the child;
(8) The responsibility of the parents for the support of others; and
(9) The value of the services contributed by the custodial parent.

Section 16. Costs.—The court may order reasonable fees for counsel, experts, the child's guardian ad litem, and other costs of the action and pre-trial proceedings, including blood tests, to be paid by the parties in such proportions and at such times as determined by the court, except that:

(1) No fees or costs shall be assessed to an indigent party prior to final adjudication of paternity or as a condition precedent to blood tests; and

(2) No such costs, other than the costs of blood tests and any other fees or charges assessed pursuant to subsection 4 of section 11 of this act, shall be assessed to the state of Missouri or a political subdivision thereof.

Section 17. Enforcement of judgment or order—payments to be made to circuit clerk—failure to comply, civil contempt.—1. If the existence of a parent and child relationship is declared, and a duty of support has been established under sections 1 to 24 of this act, the support obligation may be enforced in the same or in other appropriate proceedings by the mother, the child, the division of child support enforcement, or any other public agency that has furnished or may furnish the reasonable expenses of pregnancy, confinement, education, support, or funeral, or by any other person, including a private agency, to the extent he has furnished or is furnishing these expenses.

2. The court shall order that support payments be made to the clerk of the circuit court as trustee for remittance to the person entitled to receive the payments, or where that person has assigned his support rights to the division of family services under section 208.040, RSMo, as trustee for remittance to the division, as long as the trusteeship remains in effect.

3. Willful failure to obey any judgment or order of the court entered under this section is a civil contempt of court. Section 452.350, RSMo, applies to support orders entered under this section, and all administrative and judicial remedies for the enforcements of judgments shall apply.

Section 18. Modification of judgment or order.—The court has continuing jurisdiction to modify a judgment or order entered under sections 1 to 24 of this act. Support orders are modifiable prospectively, as provided by section 452.370, RSMo.

Section 19. Hearings and records, confidentiality.—Notwithstanding any other law concerning public hearings and records, any hearing or trial held under sections 1 to 24 of this act shall be held in closed court without admittance of any person other than those necessary to the action or proceeding. All papers and records, other than

Figure 36: *Laws*, Sec. 17, p.652 (Mo., 1987)

Montana

Montana Code Annotated § 40-6-116(3)(c) *(Judgment or order; "Uniform Parentage Act" Acts 1975 No. 512 § 16 p.1372 as Revised Codes § 61-316(3))*

The judgment or order may direct the father to pay the reasonable expenses of the mother's pregnancy and confinement.

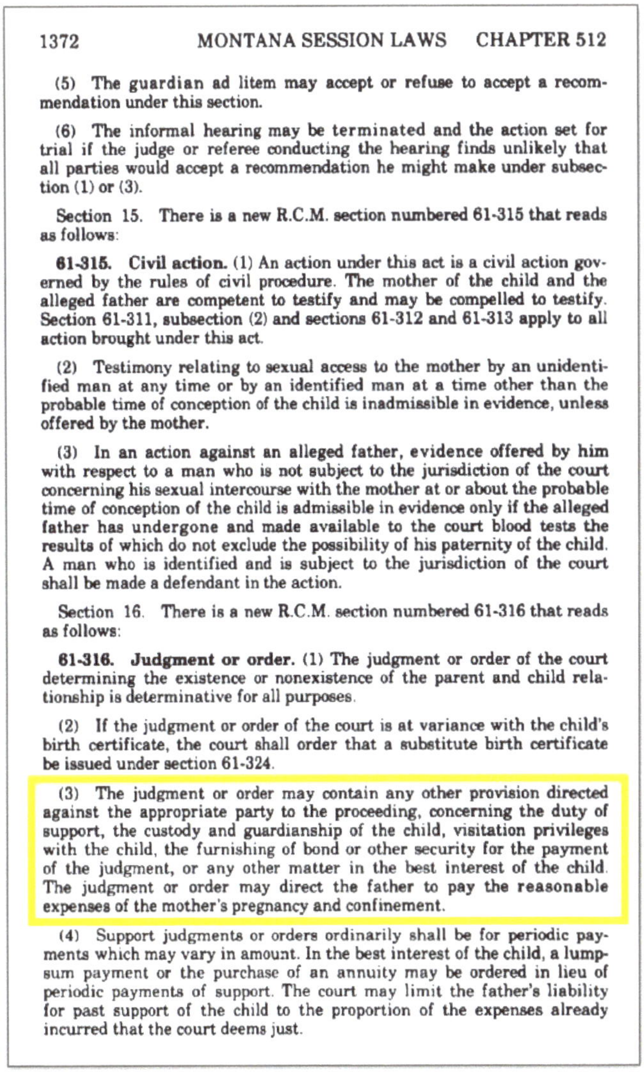

1372 MONTANA SESSION LAWS CHAPTER 512

(5) The guardian ad litem may accept or refuse to accept a recommendation under this section.

(6) The informal hearing may be terminated and the action set for trial if the judge or referee conducting the hearing finds unlikely that all parties would accept a recommendation he might make under subsection (1) or (3).

Section 15. There is a new R.C.M. section numbered 61-315 that reads as follows:

61-315. Civil action. (1) An action under this act is a civil action governed by the rules of civil procedure. The mother of the child and the alleged father are competent to testify and may be compelled to testify. Section 61-311, subsection (2) and sections 61-312 and 61-313 apply to all action brought under this act.

(2) Testimony relating to sexual access to the mother by an unidentified man at any time or by an identified man at a time other than the probable time of conception of the child is inadmissible in evidence, unless offered by the mother.

(3) In an action against an alleged father, evidence offered by him with respect to a man who is not subject to the jurisdiction of the court concerning his sexual intercourse with the mother at or about the probable time of conception of the child is admissible in evidence only if the alleged father has undergone and made available to the court blood tests the results of which do not exclude the possibility of his paternity of the child. A man who is identified and is subject to the jurisdiction of the court shall be made a defendant in the action.

Section 16. There is a new R.C.M. section numbered 61-316 that reads as follows:

61-316. Judgment or order. (1) The judgment or order of the court determining the existence or nonexistence of the parent and child relationship is determinative for all purposes.

(2) If the judgment or order of the court is at variance with the child's birth certificate, the court shall order that a substitute birth certificate be issued under section 61-324.

(3) The judgment or order may contain any other provision directed against the appropriate party to the proceeding, concerning the duty of support, the custody and guardianship of the child, visitation privileges with the child, the furnishing of bond or other security for the payment of the judgment, or any other matter in the best interest of the child. The judgment or order may direct the father to pay the reasonable expenses of the mother's pregnancy and confinement.

(4) Support judgments or orders ordinarily shall be for periodic payments which may vary in amount. In the best interest of the child, a lump-sum payment or the purchase of an annuity may be ordered in lieu of periodic payments of support. The court may limit the father's liability for past support of the child to the proportion of the expenses already incurred that the court deems just.

Figure 37: *Session Laws*, no.512 (Mont., 1975)

Revised Codes § 16-325(3) *(Custodial proceedings; "Uniform Parentage Act" Acts 1975 No. 512 § 25 p.1375)*

In an effort to identify the natural father, the court shall cause inquiry to be made of the mother and any other appropriate person. The inquiry shall include the following: whether the mother was married at the time of conception of the child or at any time thereafter; whether the mother was cohabiting with a man at the time of conception or birth of the child; **whether the mother has received support payments or promises of support with respect to the child or in connection with her pregnancy**; or whether any man has formally or informally acknowledged or declared his possible paternity of the child. Notwithstanding this section or any other provision of law and in consideration of her right to privacy, no mother of a child subject to proceedings under this act may be compelled to testify to, or divulge the identify of, the father or possible father of that child.

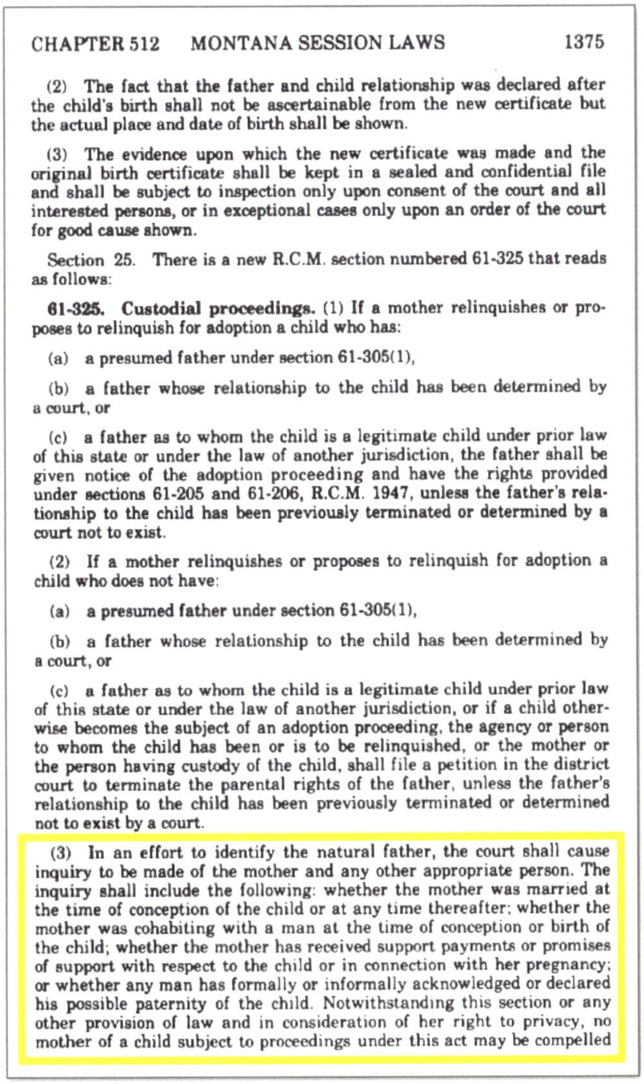

CHAPTER 512 MONTANA SESSION LAWS 1375

(2) The fact that the father and child relationship was declared after the child's birth shall not be ascertainable from the new certificate but the actual place and date of birth shall be shown.

(3) The evidence upon which the new certificate was made and the original birth certificate shall be kept in a sealed and confidential file and shall be subject to inspection only upon consent of the court and all interested persons, or in exceptional cases only upon an order of the court for good cause shown.

Section 25. There is a new R.C.M. section numbered 61-325 that reads as follows:

61-325. Custodial proceedings. (1) If a mother relinquishes or proposes to relinquish for adoption a child who has:

(a) a presumed father under section 61-305(1),

(b) a father whose relationship to the child has been determined by a court, or

(c) a father as to whom the child is a legitimate child under prior law of this state or under the law of another jurisdiction, the father shall be given notice of the adoption proceeding and have the rights provided under sections 61-205 and 61-206, R.C.M. 1947, unless the father's relationship to the child has been previously terminated or determined by a court not to exist.

(2) If a mother relinquishes or proposes to relinquish for adoption a child who does not have:

(a) a presumed father under section 61-305(1),

(b) a father whose relationship to the child has been determined by a court, or

(c) a father as to whom the child is a legitimate child under prior law of this state or under the law of another jurisdiction, or if a child otherwise becomes the subject of an adoption proceeding, the agency or person to whom the child has been or is to be relinquished, or the mother or the person having custody of the child, shall file a petition in the district court to terminate the parental rights of the father, unless the father's relationship to the child has been previously terminated or determined not to exist by a court.

(3) In an effort to identify the natural father, the court shall cause inquiry to be made of the mother and any other appropriate person. The inquiry shall include the following: whether the mother was married at the time of conception of the child or at any time thereafter; whether the mother was cohabiting with a man at the time of conception or birth of the child; whether the mother has received support payments or promises of support with respect to the child or in connection with her pregnancy; or whether any man has formally or informally acknowledged or declared his possible paternity of the child. Notwithstanding this section or any other provision of law and in consideration of her right to privacy, no mother of a child subject to proceedings under this act may be compelled

Figure 38: *Session Laws*, No.512 (Mont., 1975)

Nebraska

The earliest reference to prenatal child support in Nebraska came with the 1893 court case *Hanisky v. Kennedy*[29]. The case was filed while Hanisky was pregnant but could not be convened until the next term of the District Court, five months later. Within that timespan, the child was born and died after a month. As cited in the *Compiled Statutes of Nebraska* (1922), this case established that "maintenance" includes "expenses of confinement." The first codified law to outline applicable support requirements did not come for forty-eight years, in 1941.

Nebraska Revised Statutes § 43-1407 *(liability of father; Laws 1941 ch.81)*
The father of a child shall also be liable for the reasonable expenses of the mother of such child during the period of her **pregnancy, confinement, and recovery**. Such liability shall be determined and enforced in the same manner as the liability of the father for the support of the child.

Nebraska Revised Statutes § 43-1407(1) *(liability of father; LB 554 § 43, 2007, section split)*
The father of a child shall also be liable for the reasonable expenses of (a) the child that are associated with the **birth** of the child and (b) the mother of such child during the period of her **pregnancy, confinement, and recovery**. Such liability shall be determined and enforced in the same manner as the liability of the father for the support of the child.

Nebraska Revised Statutes § 43-104.01(2)(e) *(Child born out of wedlock; LB 594, 1999, as 43-104.03; LB 247, 2007)*
a statement by the putative father that he acknowledges liability for contribution to the support and education of the child after birth and for contribution to the **pregnancy-related medical expenses of the mother** of the child. The person filing the notice shall notify the registry of any change of address pursuant to procedures prescribed in rules and regulations of the department.

Nebraska Revised Statutes § 43-104.13(7) *(Child born out of wedlock; LB 712, 1995)*
That if he is the biological father and if the child is not relinquished for adoption, he has a duty to contribute to the support and education of the child and to the **pregnancy-related expenses of the mother** and a right to seek a court order for custody, parenting time, visitation, or other access with the child.

Figure 39: *Session Laws*, ch.81 (Neb., 1941)

Nebraska Revised Statutes § 43-104.19 *(Child born out of wedlock; LB 712, 1995)*
The guardian ad litem for the biological father shall:... (4) Determine, by deposition, by affidavit, by interview, or through testimony at a hearing, the following: Whether the mother was married at the time of conception of the child or at any time thereafter, whether the mother was cohabitating with a man at the time of conception or birth of the child, whether the mother has received **support payments or promises of support** with respect to the child or **in connection with her pregnancy**, whether conception was the result of sexual assault or incest, and whether any man has formally or informally acknowledged or declared his possible paternity of the child.

Nebraska Revised Statutes § 43-104.22(5) *(Child born out of wedlock; LB 712, 1995, split from (4) in LB 594, 1999)*
The father had knowledge of the pregnancy and failed to **provide reasonable support for the mother during the pregnancy**

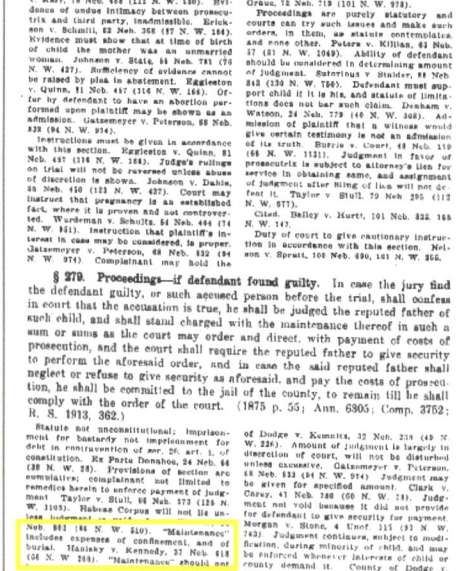

Figure 40: Ref to *Hanisky v. Kennedy*

Nevada

Revised Statutes § 125B.020(3) *(Obligation of parents; Laws 1923 ch.87; re-enacted in SB 472, 1983)*

1. The parents of a child (in this chapter referred to as "the child") have a duty to provide the child necessary maintenance, health care, education and support.
2. They are also liable, in the event of the child's death, for its funeral expenses.
3. **The father is also liable to pay the expenses of the mother's pregnancy and confinement.**
4. The obligation of the parent to support the child under the laws for the support of poor relatives applies to children born out of wedlock.

Revised Statutes § 125B.080(9)(h) *(Amount of payment; AB 424, 1987 as 125B.080(8)(h); renumbered to 125B.080(9)(h) in 1989 ch.859)*

Any **expenses reasonably related to the mother's pregnancy and confinement**

Revised Statutes § 126.161(4)(b) *(Contents and effect of judgment or order.; 1979 Statues ch.599 sec.17 p.1275; SB 294)*

Direct the father to pay the **reasonable expenses of the mother's pregnancy and confinement**. The court may limit the father's liability for past support of the child to the proportion of the expenses already incurred which the court deems just.

Revised Statutes § 126.181(1) *(Enforcement of judgment or order; 1979 Statues ch.599 sec.19 p.1276; SB 294)*

If the parent and child relationship has been established, the obligation of a parent may be enforced in the same or independent proceedings by the other parent, the child, the public authority that has furnished or may furnish the **reasonable expenses of pregnancy, confinement**, education, support or funeral, or by any other person, including a private agency, to the extent he or she has furnished or is furnishing these expenses.

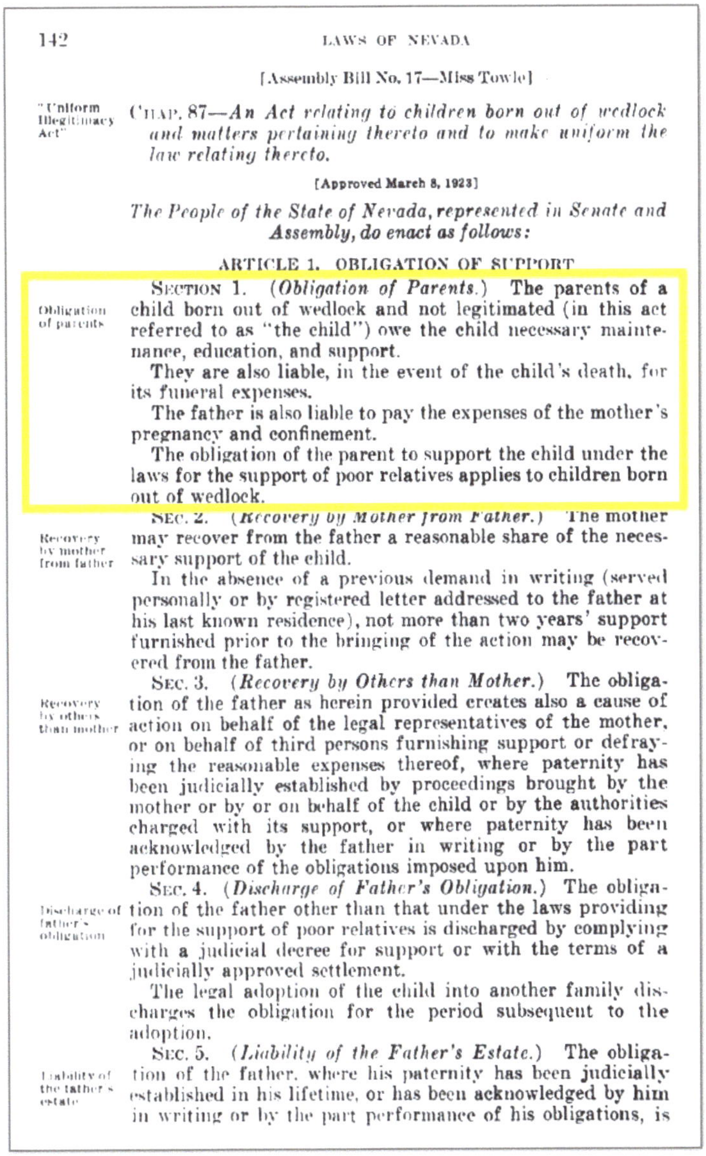

142 LAWS OF NEVADA

[Assembly Bill No. 17—Miss Towle]

"Uniform Illegitimacy Act"

CHAP. 87—*An Act relating to children born out of wedlock and matters pertaining thereto and to make uniform the law relating thereto.*

[Approved March 8, 1923]

The People of the State of Nevada, represented in Senate and Assembly, do enact as follows:

ARTICLE 1. OBLIGATION OF SUPPORT

Obligation of parents

SECTION 1. (*Obligation of Parents.*) The parents of a child born out of wedlock and not legitimated (in this act referred to as "the child") owe the child necessary maintenance, education, and support.

They are also liable, in the event of the child's death, for its funeral expenses.

The father is also liable to pay the expenses of the mother's pregnancy and confinement.

The obligation of the parent to support the child under the laws for the support of poor relatives applies to children born out of wedlock.

Recovery by mother from father

SEC. 2. (*Recovery by Mother from Father.*) The mother may recover from the father a reasonable share of the necessary support of the child.

In the absence of a previous demand in writing (served personally or by registered letter addressed to the father at his last known residence), not more than two years' support furnished prior to the bringing of the action may be recovered from the father.

Recovery by others than mother

SEC. 3. (*Recovery by Others than Mother.*) The obligation of the father as herein provided creates also a cause of action on behalf of the legal representatives of the mother, or on behalf of third persons furnishing support or defraying the reasonable expenses thereof, where paternity has been judicially established by proceedings brought by the mother or by or on behalf of the child or by the authorities charged with its support, or where paternity has been acknowledged by the father in writing or by the part performance of the obligations imposed upon him.

Discharge of father's obligation

SEC. 4. (*Discharge of Father's Obligation.*) The obligation of the father other than that under the laws providing for the support of poor relatives is discharged by complying with a judicial decree for support or with the terms of a judicially approved settlement.

The legal adoption of the child into another family discharges the obligation for the period subsequent to the adoption.

Liability of the father's estate

SEC. 5. (*Liability of the Father's Estate.*) The obligation of the father, where his paternity has been judicially established in his lifetime, or has been acknowledged by him in writing or by the part performance of his obligations, is

Figure 41: *Laws*, ch.87 (Nevada, 1923)

Revised Statutes § 126.201(1) *(Right to counsel; SB 472, 1983)*

At the pretrial hearing and in further proceedings, any party may be represented by counsel. If a party is financially unable to obtain counsel, the court may appoint counsel to represent that party with respect to the determination of the existence or nonexistence of the parent and child relationship and the duty of support, including without limitation the **expenses of the mother's pregnancy and confinement, medical expenses for the birth of the child** and support of the child from birth until trial.

New Hampshire

Revised Statutes Annotated § 168-A:1 *(Obligation of the Father, enforcement; Uniform Act on Paternity, PL 1971 ch.530)*

The father of a child which is or may be born of unwed parents is liable to the same extent as the father of a child born in wedlock, whether or not the child is born alive, for the **reasonable expense of the mother's pregnancy and confinement** and for the education and necessary support of the child. A child born of unwed parents includes a child born to a married woman by a man other than her husband.

Revised Statutes Annotated § 168-A:2(VI) *(Establishment of Paternity, enforcement; Uniform Act on Paternity, PL 1971 ch.530)*

Copies of **bills for pregnancy, childbirth**, and genetic paternity testing shall be admissible as evidence without requiring third-party foundation testimony, and shall constitute prima facie evidence of costs incurred for such services or for genetic paternity testing.

Revised Statutes Annotated § 168-A:4(I) *(Remedies; Uniform Act on Paternity, PL 1971 ch.530)*

The superior court has jurisdiction of a proceeding under this chapter and all remedies for the enforcement of judgments for **expenses of pregnancy and confinement for a mother** or for education or necessary support of children apply including, but not limited to, the provisions of RSA 161-B, 161-C, and 458.

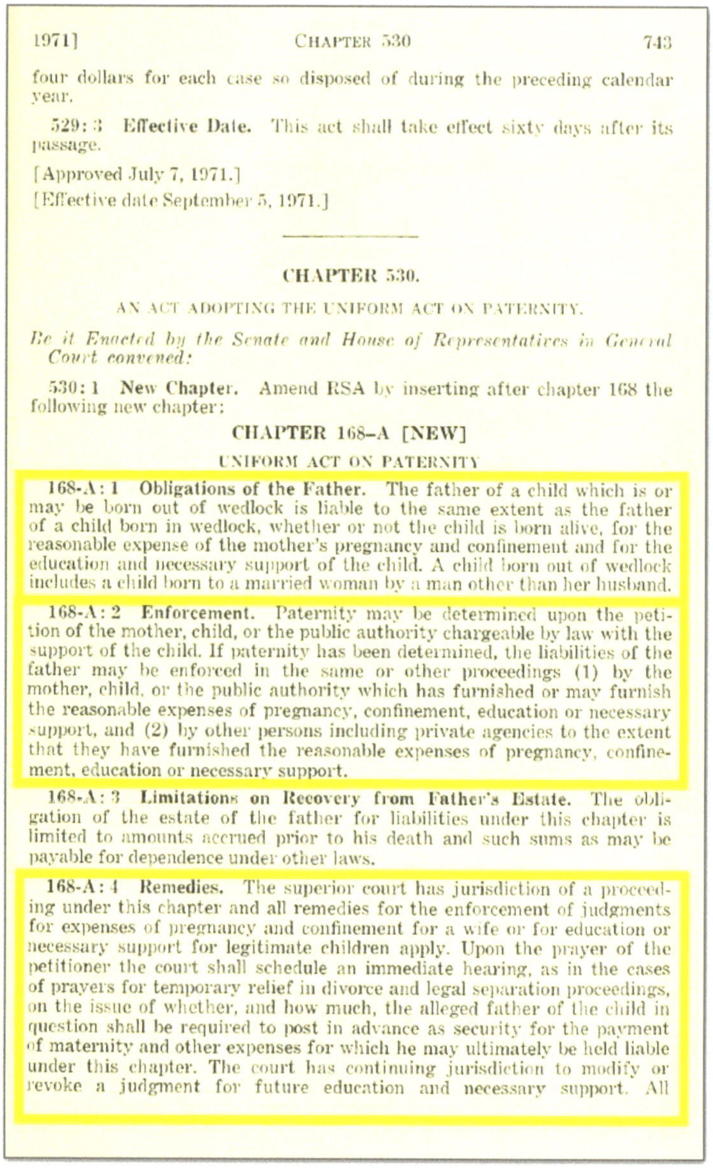

1971] CHAPTER 530 743

four dollars for each case so disposed of during the preceding calendar year.

529:3 **Effective Date.** This act shall take effect sixty days after its passage.

[Approved July 7, 1971.]

[Effective date September 5, 1971.]

CHAPTER 530.

AN ACT ADOPTING THE UNIFORM ACT ON PATERNITY.

Be it Enacted by the Senate and House of Representatives in General Court convened:

530:1 **New Chapter.** Amend RSA by inserting after chapter 168 the following new chapter:

CHAPTER 168–A [NEW]

UNIFORM ACT ON PATERNITY

168-A:1 **Obligations of the Father.** The father of a child which is or may be born out of wedlock is liable to the same extent as the father of a child born in wedlock, whether or not the child is born alive, for the reasonable expense of the mother's pregnancy and confinement and for the education and necessary support of the child. A child born out of wedlock includes a child born to a married woman by a man other than her husband.

168-A:2 **Enforcement.** Paternity may be determined upon the petition of the mother, child, or the public authority chargeable by law with the support of the child. If paternity has been determined, the liabilities of the father may be enforced in the same or other proceedings (1) by the mother, child, or the public authority which has furnished or may furnish the reasonable expenses of pregnancy, confinement, education or necessary support, and (2) by other persons including private agencies to the extent that they have furnished the reasonable expenses of pregnancy, confinement, education or necessary support.

168-A:3 **Limitations on Recovery from Father's Estate.** The obligation of the estate of the father for liabilities under this chapter is limited to amounts accrued prior to his death and such sums as may be payable for dependence under other laws.

168-A:4 **Remedies.** The superior court has jurisdiction of a proceeding under this chapter and all remedies for the enforcement of judgments for expenses of pregnancy and confinement for a wife or for education or necessary support for legitimate children apply. Upon the prayer of the petitioner the court shall schedule an immediate hearing, as in the cases of prayers for temporary relief in divorce and legal separation proceedings, on the issue of whether, and how much, the alleged father of the child in question shall be required to post in advance as security for the payment of maternity and other expenses for which he may ultimately be held liable under this chapter. The court has continuing jurisdiction to modify or revoke a judgment for future education and necessary support. All

Figure 42: *Public Laws*, ch.530 (NH, 1971)

New Jersey

New Jersey had quite a rabbit hole of legislation. The 1888 session law on this page referenced legislation from 1846 and 1864. The latter contained no changes for the applicable section, and the former turned out being the *Revised Statutes of 1846*. These contained no applicable changes but further referenced the 1840-1 session. This session did not even include bastardy legislation, but beyond the index for the year's volume was a short second session with further legislation that referenced the initial 1795 *An Act for the Maintenance of Bastard Children*. This act had nothing applicable to prenatal child support, leaving the 1888 session law as the earliest instance.

Revision of the Statutes of New Jersey, 1887, Unclear code section
(Order of filiation; L. 1888 ch. LXVIII)
...for any breaches of such bond which shall happen after the recovery of any damages or the commencement of any suit, a scire facias may issue, upon which the damages shall be assessed from time to time in manner aforesaid : and all moneys which shall be collected on such bond shall be paid to such township or townships as may have incurred or been put to **expense in supporting said bastard, or its mother during her confinement, or from costs therefrom arising.**

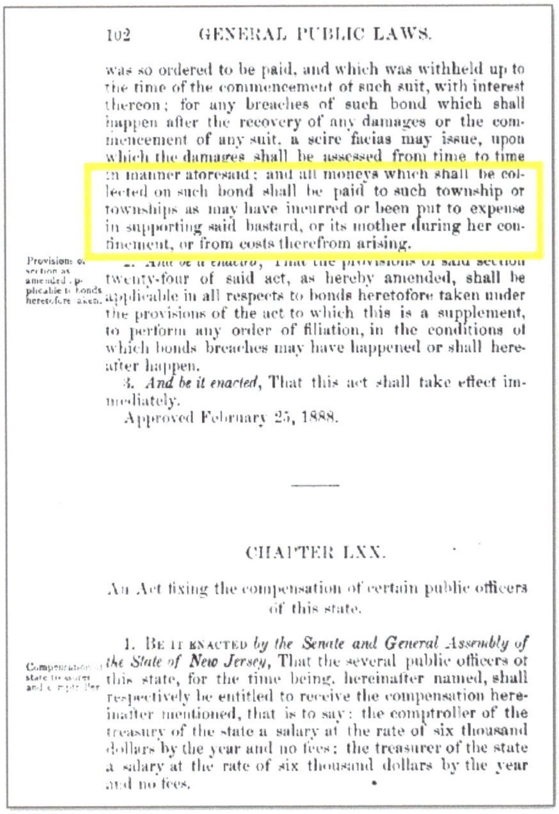

102 GENERAL PUBLIC LAWS.

was so ordered to be paid, and which was withheld up to the time of the commencement of such suit, with interest thereon; for any breaches of such bond which shall happen after the recovery of any damages or the commencement of any suit, a scire facias may issue, upon which the damages shall be assessed from time to time in manner aforesaid; and all moneys which shall be collected on such bond shall be paid to such township or townships as may have incurred or been put to expense in supporting said bastard, or its mother during her confinement, or from costs therefrom arising.

Provisions of section as amended applicable to bonds heretofore taken.

2. And be it enacted, That the provisions of said section twenty-four of said act, as hereby amended, shall be applicable in all respects to bonds heretofore taken under the provisions of the act to which this is a supplement, to perform any order of filiation, in the conditions of which bonds breaches may have happened or shall hereafter happen.

3. *And be it enacted*, That this act shall take effect immediately.

Approved February 25, 1888.

CHAPTER LXX.

An Act fixing the compensation of certain public officers of this state.

Compensation of state treasurer and comptroller.

1. BE IT ENACTED *by the Senate and General Assembly of the State of New Jersey*, That the several public officers of this state, for the time being, hereinafter named, shall respectively be entitled to receive the compensation hereinafter mentioned, that is to say: the comptroller of the treasury of the state a salary at the rate of six thousand dollars by the year and no fees; the treasurer of the state a salary at the rate of six thousand dollars by the year and no fees.

Figure 43: *General Public Laws*, ch. LXVIII (NJ, 1888)

New Jersey Statutes Annotated § 9:17-53(16)(c) *(Judgment; L 1983 ch.17)*
The judgment or order may contain any other provision directed against the appropriate party to the proceeding concerning the duty of support , the custody and guardianship of the child , parenting time privileges with the child , the furnishing of bond or other security for the payment of the judgment, the repayment of any public assistance grant, or any other matter in the best interests of the child . The judgment or order may direct the father to pay the **reasonable expenses of the mother's pregnancy** and postpartum disability, including repayment to an agency which provided public assistance funds for those expenses. Bills for pregnancy, childbirth and blood or genetic testing are admissible as evidence without requiring third party foundation testimony, and shall constitute prima facie evidence of the amounts incurred for these services or for testing on behalf of the child

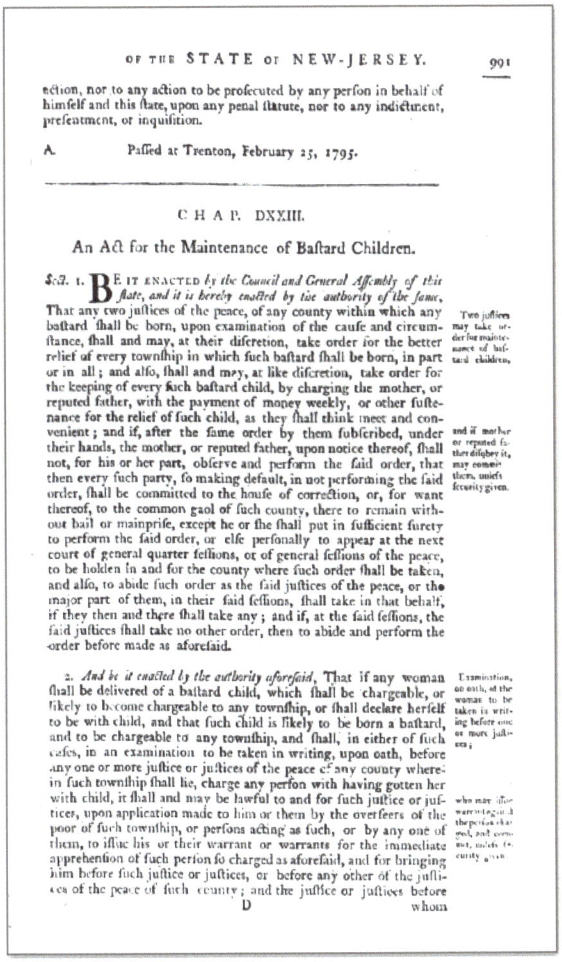

OF THE STATE OF NEW-JERSEY. 991

ection, nor to any action to be profecuted by any perfon in behalf of himfelf and this ftate, upon any penal ftatute, nor to any indictment, prefentment, or inquifition.

A. Paffed at Trenton, February 25, 1795.

C H A P. DXXIII.

An Act for the Maintenance of Baftard Children.

Two juftices may take order for maintenance of baftard children,

Sect. 1. BE IT ENACTED *by the Council and General Affembly of this ftate, and it is hereby enacted by the authority of the fame*, That any two juftices of the peace, of any county within which any baftard fhall be born, upon examination of the caufe and circumftance, fhall and may, at their difcretion, take order for the better relief of every townfhip in which fuch baftard fhall be born, in part or in all; and alfo, fhall and may, at like difcretion, take order for the keeping of every fuch baftard child, by charging the mother, or reputed father, with the payment of money weekly, or other fuftenance for the relief of fuch child, as they fhall think meet and convenient; and if, after the fame order by them fubfcribed, under their hands, the mother, or reputed father, upon notice thereof, fhall not, for his or her part, obferve and perform the faid order, that then every fuch party, fo making default, in not performing the faid order, fhall be committed to the houfe of correction, or, for want thereof, to the common gaol of fuch county, there to remain without bail or mainprife, except he or fhe fhall put in fufficient furety to perform the faid order, or elfe perfonally to appear at the next court of general quarter feffions, or of general feffions of the peace, to be holden in and for the county where fuch order fhall be taken, and alfo, to abide fuch order as the faid juftices of the peace, or the major part of them, in their faid feffions, fhall take in that behalf, if they then and there fhall take any; and if, at the faid feffions, the faid juftices fhall take no other order, then to abide and perform the order before made as aforefaid.

and if mother or reputed father difobey it, may commit them, unlefs fecurity given.

Examination, on oath, of the woman to be taken in writing before one or more juftices;

2. *And be it enacted by the authority aforefaid*, That if any woman fhall be delivered of a baftard child, which fhall be chargeable, or likely to become chargeable to any townfhip, or fhall declare herfelf to be with child, and that fuch child is likely to be born a baftard, and to be chargeable to any townfhip, and fhall, in either of fuch cafes, in an examination to be taken in writing, upon oath, before any one or more juftice or juftices of the peace of any county wherein fuch townfhip fhall lie, charge any perfon with having gotten her with child, it fhall and may be lawful to and for fuch juftice or juftices, upon application made to him or them by the overfeers of the poor of fuch townfhip, or perfons acting as fuch, or by any one of them, to iffue his or their warrant or warrants for the immediate apprehenfion of fuch perfon fo charged as aforefaid, and for bringing him before fuch juftice or juftices, or before any other of the juftices of the peace of fuch county; and the juftice or juftices before

who may iffue warrant againft the perfon charged, and commit, unlefs fecurity given.

D whom

Figure 44: *Acts*, ch. DXXIII (NJ, 1795)

New Jersey Statutes Annotated § 9:17-55(18)(a) *(Enforcing parties; L 1983 ch.17)*
If existence of the father and child relationship is declared, or paternity or a duty of support has been acknowledged or adjudicated under this act or under prior law, the obligation of the father may be enforced in the same or other proceedings by the mother, and child, the public agency that has furnished or may furnish the **reasonable expenses of pregnancy**, postpartum disability, education, support, medical expenses, or burial, or by any other person, including a private agency, to the extent that the mother, child, person or agency has furnished or is furnishing these expenses.

New Mexico

Though the title is never used, New Mexico's 1923 "An Act Relating to Children Born Out of Wedlock" appears to be the state's implementation of the *Uniform Illegitimacy Act* that several other states passed the same year.

New Mexico Statutes Annotated, Superseded Code Section *(An Act Relating to Children Born Out of Wedlock; Laws 1923 ch. 32 § 2)*
The father owes the child maintenance and support, having regard to the condition in life of the mother, until the child attains the age of sixteen years, or the child physically or mentally incapable of working, until the child arrives at full age. **The father is also liable to pay the expenses of the mother's pregnancy and confinement.** The father also liable for the child funeral expenses.

New Mexico Statutes Annotated § 40-11A-636(G) *(Order adjudicating parentage; SB463, 2009)*
The judgment or order may contain any other provision directed against or on behalf of the appropriate party to the proceeding concerning the duty of past and future support, the custody and guardianship of the child, visitation with the child, the furnishing of bond or other security for the payment of the judgment or any other matter within the jurisdiction of the court. The judgment or order may direct the father to pay the **reasonable expenses of the mother's pregnancy, birth and confinement**. The court shall order child support retroactive to the date of the child's birth, but not to exceed twelve years unless there is a substantial showing that paternity could not have been established and an action for child support could not have been brought within twelve years of the child's birth pursuant to the provisions of Sections 40-4-11 through 40-4-11.3 NMSA 1978; provided that, in deciding whether or how long to order retroactive support, the court shall consider...

CHAP. 32 LAWS OF 1923 49

lock and not legitimated (in this Act referred to as "the child") maintenance and support as if the same were born in wedlock.

Sec. 2. The father owes the child maintenance and support, having regard to the condition in life of the mother, until the child attains the age of sixteen years, or if the child is physically or mentally incapable of working, until the child arrives at full age. The father is also liable to pay the expenses of the mother's pregnancy and confinement. The father is also liable for the child's funeral expenses.

Sec. 3. The mother may recover from the father an equal share of the support which she has furnished or owes to the child, or in the case of her total or partial inability, so much in addition as to make up the amount of the support she owes.

In the absence of a previous demand in writing (served personally or by registered letter addressed to the father at his last known residence), not more than two years' support furnished prior to the bringing of the action can be recovered from the father.

Sec. 4. The obligation of the father creates also a cause of action on behalf of the legal representatives of the mother, or on behalf of third parties furnishing support or defraying the expenses thereof where paternity has been judicially established, or where paternity has been acknowledged by him in writing or by the part performance of the obligations imposed upon him.

Sec. 5. The obligation of the father is discharged by complying with a judicial decree for support or with the terms of a judicially approved settlement. The adoption of the child into another family discharges the obligation for the period subsequent to the adoption.

Sec. 6. The obligation of the father, where his paternity has been judicially established in his life time, or has been acknowledged by him in writing or by the part performance of his obligations, is enforceable against his estate, subject and subordinate to the like claims to support in favor of the widow and lawful children. The Court may direct the discharge of the obligation by periodical payments or by the payment of a lump sum.

Sec. 7. Proceedings to compel support by the father provided herein, shall not be exclusive of other proceedings that may be available on principles of law or equity.

Sec. 8. The proceeding to compel support may be brought by the mother, or if the child is or is likely to be a public charge, by the Attorney General, or any District Attorney, in the name of the State of New Mexico. After the death of the mother or

Figure 45: *Laws*, ch.32, sec.2 (NM, 1923)

New York

Revised Statutes of 1929, Chap. XX, Title 6, § 14 *(Of the support of bastards; 1828)*

Such person, so adjudged to be the reputed father, shall, upon notice of such order, immediately pay the amount so certified for the costs of apprehending him, and of the order of filiation; and shall enter into a bond to the people of this state, in such sum as such justices shall direct, with good and sufficient sureties, to be approved by them, with one or other of the following conditions: First, that such person will pay weekly, or otherwise, as shall have been ordered, such sum for the support of the said child, and for the sustenance of its mother as aforesaid, as shall have been ordered, or shall at any time thereafter be ordered by the court of general sessions of the peace of the same county; and that he will fully and amply indemnify the county and town, or city, where the said bastard shall have been born, or where the woman likely to have such bastard shall be, and every other county, town or city, which may have incurred any expense, or may be put to **any expense for the support of such child, or its mother, during her confinement and recovery therefrom, against all such expenses**: Or, second, that such person will appear at the next court of general sessions of the peace of the said county, and not depart the said court, without its leave.

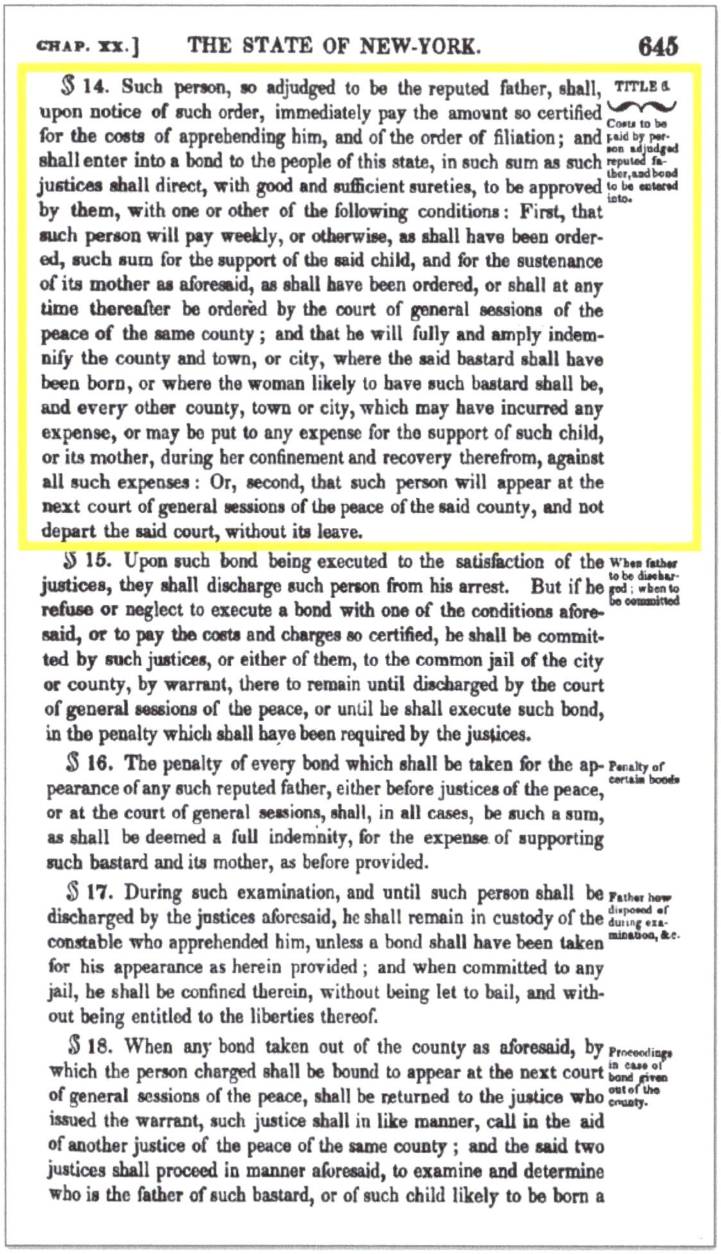
CHAP. XX.] THE STATE OF NEW-YORK. 645

§ 14. Such person, so adjudged to be the reputed father, shall, upon notice of such order, immediately pay the amount so certified for the costs of apprehending him, and of the order of filiation; and shall enter into a bond to the people of this state, in such sum as such justices shall direct, with good and sufficient sureties, to be approved by them, with one or other of the following conditions: First, that such person will pay weekly, or otherwise, as shall have been ordered, such sum for the support of the said child, and for the sustenance of its mother as aforesaid, as shall have been ordered, or shall at any time thereafter be ordered by the court of general sessions of the peace of the same county; and that he will fully and amply indemnify the county and town, or city, where the said bastard shall have been born, or where the woman likely to have such bastard shall be, and every other county, town or city, which may have incurred any expense, or may be put to any expense for the support of such child, or its mother, during her confinement and recovery therefrom, against all such expenses: Or, second, that such person will appear at the next court of general sessions of the peace of the said county, and not depart the said court, without its leave.

TITLE 6. Costs to be paid by person adjudged reputed father, and bond to be entered into.

§ 15. Upon such bond being executed to the satisfaction of the justices, they shall discharge such person from his arrest. But if he refuse or neglect to execute a bond with one of the conditions aforesaid, or to pay the costs and charges so certified, he shall be committed by such justices, or either of them, to the common jail of the city or county, by warrant, there to remain until discharged by the court of general sessions of the peace, or until he shall execute such bond, in the penalty which shall have been required by the justices.

When father to be discharged; when to be committed

§ 16. The penalty of every bond which shall be taken for the appearance of any such reputed father, either before justices of the peace, or at the court of general sessions, shall, in all cases, be such a sum, as shall be deemed a full indemnity, for the expense of supporting such bastard and its mother, as before provided.

Penalty of certain bonds

§ 17. During such examination, and until such person shall be discharged by the justices aforesaid, he shall remain in custody of the constable who apprehended him, unless a bond shall have been taken for his appearance as herein provided; and when committed to any jail, he shall be confined therein, without being let to bail, and without being entitled to the liberties thereof.

Father how disposed of during examination, &c.

§ 18. When any bond taken out of the county as aforesaid, by which the person charged shall be bound to appear at the next court of general sessions of the peace, shall be returned to the justice who issued the warrant, such justice shall in like manner, call in the aid of another justice of the peace of the same county; and the said two justices shall proceed in manner aforesaid, to examine and determine who is the father of such bastard, or of such child likely to be born a

Proceedings in case of bond given out of the county.

Figure 46: *Laws*, Chap. XX, Title 6, § 14 (NY, 1828)

New York FCT § 5-514 *(Liability of father to mother; 1962 ch.686)*

The father is liable for the **reasonable expenses of the mother's confinement and recovery and such reasonable expenses in connection with her pregnancy** as determined by the court; provided, however, where the mother's confinement, recovery and expenses in connection with her pregnancy were paid under the medical assistance program on the mother's behalf, the father may be liable to the social services district furnishing such medical assistance and to the state department of health for medical assistance so expended. Such expenses, including such expenses paid by the medical assistance program on the mother's behalf, shall be deemed cash medical support and the court shall determine the obligation of the parties to contribute to the cost thereof pursuant to subparagraph five of paragraph (c) of subdivision one of section four hundred thirteen of this act.

New York FCT § 5-545 *(Injury to pregnant woman; 1962 ch.686)*

The necessary **expenses incurred by or for the mother in connection with her confinement and recovery and such expenses in connection with the pregnancy of the mother** shall be deemed cash medical support, and the court shall determine the obligation of either or both parents to contribute to the cost thereof pursuant to subparagraph five of paragraph (c) of subdivision one of section four hundred thirteen of this act.

North Carolina

North Carolina General Statutes § 49-15 *(Custody and support of children born out of wedlock when paternity established; SL 1967 ch.993)*
Upon and after the establishment of paternity pursuant to G.S. 49-14 of a child born out of wedlock, the rights, duties, and obligations of the mother and the father so established, with regard to support and custody of the child, shall be the same, and may be determined and enforced in the same manner, as if the child were the legitimate child of the father and mother. When paternity has been established, the father becomes responsible for **medical expenses incident to the pregnancy and the birth of the child**.

North Carolina General Statutes § 110-132(a3) *(Affidavit of parentage and agreement to motion to set aside affidavit of parentage; SL 1975 ch.827 as 110A-5, renumbered several times)*
A written agreement to support the child by periodic payments, which may include provision for reimbursement for **medical expenses incident to the pregnancy and the birth of the child**, accrued maintenance and reasonable expense of prosecution of the paternity action, when acknowledged as provided herein, filed with, and approved by a judge of the district court at any time, shall have the same force and effect as an order of support entered by that court, and shall be enforceable and subject to modification in the same manner as is provided by law for orders of the court in such cases.

North Carolina General Statutes § 49-14(g) *(Civil action to establish paternity; SL 1997 ch.433)*
Invoices for **services rendered for pregnancy, childbirth**, and blood or genetic testing are admissible as evidence without requiring third party foundation testimony and shall constitute prima facie evidence of the amounts incurred for the services or for testing on behalf of the child.

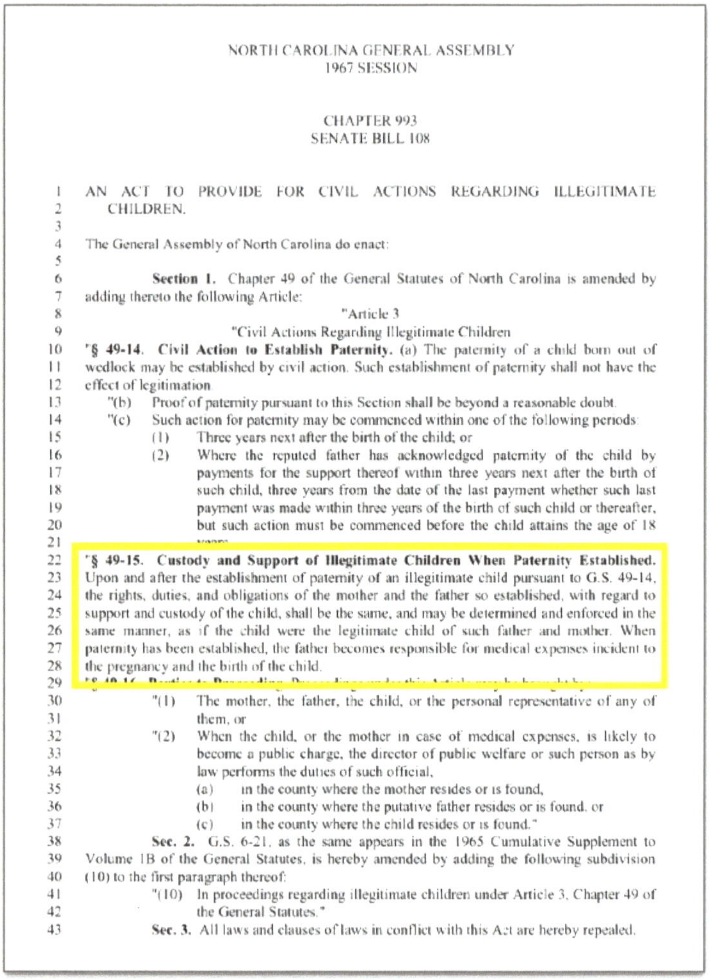

Figure 47: *Session Laws*, ch.993 (NC, 1967)

North Dakota

North Dakota's earliest applicable legislation came twenty-seven years before statehood, under the initial session of the Territory of Dakota in 1862. (For more details, see the discussion under South Dakota.)

The wording by which North Dakota's legislature enacted the *Uniform Illegitimacy Act* in 1923 led to some confusion as to how the new sections would integrate into Chapter 5A of the Compiled Laws of 1913. At the beginning of the chapter is the following explanatory note:

> This chapter, the title of which is "An act relating to children born out of wedlock and to make uniform the law with reference thereto, and for the repeal of sections 10483 to 10500 inclusive, Compiled Laws of 1913, and Chapter 70, Laws of 1917," is the Uniform Illegitimacy Act and the original act seems to have been adopted with slight changes, including the omission of § 6 of the original act and the renumbering of §§ 7-38 of the original act as §§ 6-37 of the North Dakota act. As a consequence of the renumbering. the references to other sections in §§ 29, 30, 37 are incorrect and should be as indicated in the brackets in such sections.

Due to the confusion, North Dakota's chapter numbering is the best attempt by Secretary of State Robert Byrne to apply a final *Compiled Laws* section to the Act.

Compiled Laws of 1913, Code of Criminal Procedure Chapter 5A § 10500a1 *(Uniform Illegitimacy Act; SL 1923 ch.165 § 1, SB187)*
OBLIGATION OF PARENTS.) The parents of a child born our of wedlock and not legitimated (in this act referred child "the Child") owe the child necessary maintenance, education and support. The parents are liable for the child's funeral expenses. **The father is also liable for the expenses of the mother's pregnancy and confinement.** The obligation of the parents to support the child under the laws for the support of poor relatives applies to children born out of wedlock.

Century Code § 14-20-57(4) *(Order adjudicating parentage; SL 2005 ch.135)*
The order may contain any other provision in the best interest of the child, including payment of support, payment of **expenses of the mother's pregnancy and confinement**, custody of the child, visitation with the child, and furnishing of bond or other security for payment of support. A support order must be for a monthly payment in an amount consistent with the guidelines established under section 14-09-09.7 and must be subject to section 14-09-08.1. All remedies for the enforcement of support, custody, and visitation orders apply. The court has continuing jurisdiction to modify an order for future support and, subject to section 14-09-09.6, custody of and visitation with the child.

Figure 48: *Session Laws, ch.165 (ND, 1923)*

Ohio

General Code of 1910, § 12123 *(Bastardy proceedings; SL 1923 pp.296-300, HB190)*
If, in person or by counsel, the accused Order of court when accused confesses in court that the accusation is true or, if the jury find him guilty, he shall be adjudged the reputed father of the bastard child and the court shall thereupon adjudge that he pay to the complainant such sum as the court may find to be necessary for her support, maintenance and **necessary expenses, caused by pregnancy and childbirth** together with costs of prosecution. The court shall require the reputed father to give security to perform such order...

Ohio Revised Code § 3111.13(C) *(Judgment or order; Amended* SB180, 2000*)*
Except as otherwise provided in this section, the judgment or order may contain, at the request of a party and if not prohibited under federal law, any other provision directed against the appropriate party to the proceeding, concerning the duty of support, the payment of all or any part of the **reasonable expenses of the mother's pregnancy and confinement**, the furnishing of bond or other security for the payment of the judgment, or any other matter in the best interest of the child...

Ohio Revised Code § 3111.15(A) *(Enforcing father's obligation; Amended* SB180, 2000*)*
If the existence of the father and child relationship is declared or if paternity or a duty of support has been adjudicated under sections 3111.01 to 3111.18 of the Revised Code or under prior law, the obligation of the father may be enforced in the same or other proceedings by the mother, the child, or the public authority that has furnished or may furnish the **reasonable expenses of pregnancy, confinement**, education, support, or funeral, or by any other person, including a private agency, to the extent that any of them may furnish, has furnished, or is furnishing these expenses.

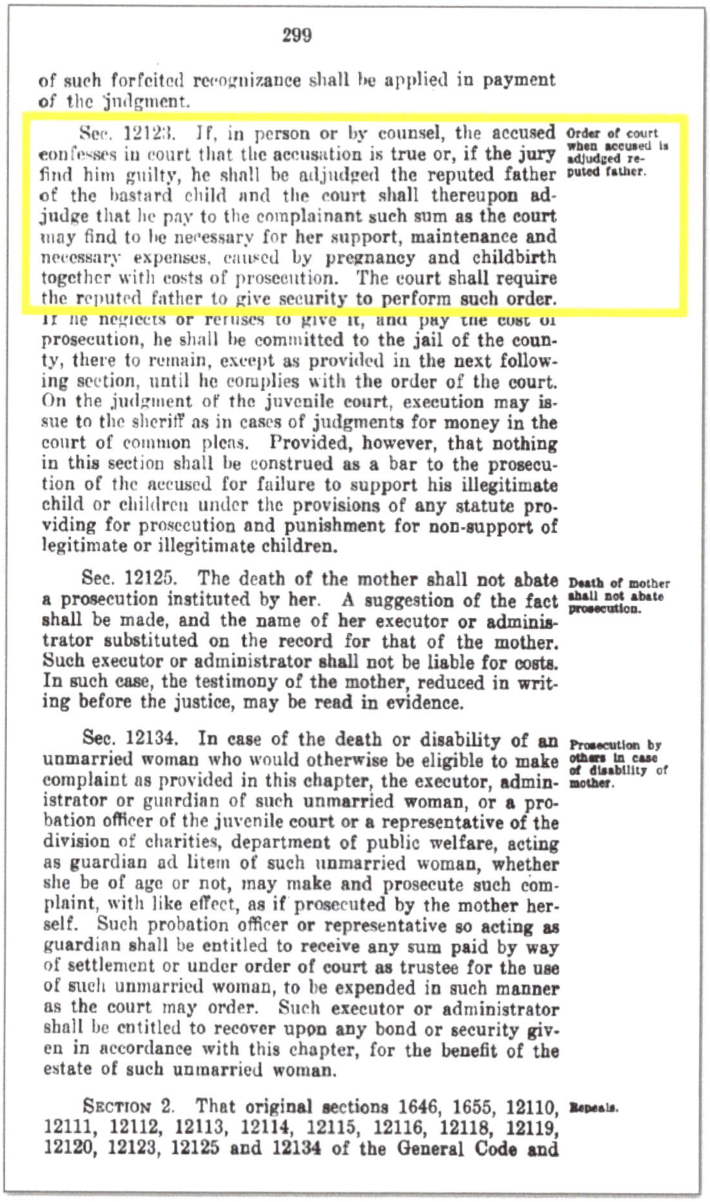

299

of such forfeited recognizance shall be applied in payment of the judgment.

Sec. 12123. If, in person or by counsel, the accused confesses in court that the accusation is true or, if the jury find him guilty, he shall be adjudged the reputed father of the bastard child and the court shall thereupon adjudge that he pay to the complainant such sum as the court may find to be necessary for her support, maintenance and necessary expenses, caused by pregnancy and childbirth together with costs of prosecution. The court shall require the reputed father to give security to perform such order. If he neglects or refuses to give it, and pay the cost of prosecution, he shall be committed to the jail of the county, there to remain, except as provided in the next following section, until he complies with the order of the court. On the judgment of the juvenile court, execution may issue to the sheriff as in cases of judgments for money in the court of common pleas. Provided, however, that nothing in this section shall be construed as a bar to the prosecution of the accused for failure to support his illegitimate child or children under the provisions of any statute providing for prosecution and punishment for non-support of legitimate or illegitimate children. — Order of court when accused is adjudged reputed father.

Sec. 12125. The death of the mother shall not abate a prosecution instituted by her. A suggestion of the fact shall be made, and the name of her executor or administrator substituted on the record for that of the mother. Such executor or administrator shall not be liable for costs. In such case, the testimony of the mother, reduced in writing before the justice, may be read in evidence. — Death of mother shall not abate prosecution.

Sec. 12134. In case of the death or disability of an unmarried woman who would otherwise be eligible to make complaint as provided in this chapter, the executor, administrator or guardian of such unmarried woman, or a probation officer of the juvenile court or a representative of the division of charities, department of public welfare, acting as guardian ad litem of such unmarried woman, whether she be of age or not, may make and prosecute such complaint, with like effect, as if prosecuted by the mother herself. Such probation officer or representative so acting as guardian shall be entitled to receive any sum paid by way of settlement or under order of court as trustee for the use of such unmarried woman, to be expended in such manner as the court may order. Such executor or administrator shall be entitled to recover upon any bond or security given in accordance with this chapter, for the benefit of the estate of such unmarried woman. — Prosecution by others in case of disability of mother.

Section 2. That original sections 1646, 1655, 12110, 12111, 12112, 12113, 12114, 12115, 12116, 12118, 12119, 12120, 12123, 12125 and 12134 of the General Code and — Repeals.

Figure 49: *Session Laws*, pp.296-300 (Ohio, 1923)

Oklahoma

10 Oklahoma Statutes §83(C) *(Liability of Father to Support and Educate Child; Laws 1965 ch.378 § 4, HB699)*

1. An individual who has been legally determined to be the father of a child pursuant to Section 70 of this title, or an individual who has been judicially or administratively determined to be the father of a child shall be ordered to pay **all or a portion of the costs of the birth** and the reasonable expenses of providing for said child or the amount of public assistance paid prior to the determination of paternity, provided that liability for support provided before the determination of paternity shall be imposed for five (5) years preceding the filing of the action.

10 Oklahoma Statutes §83(C)(2) *(Liability of Father to Support and Educate Child;* L 1997 ch. 402, SB150 - split *from §83(C))*

Copies of **bills for pregnancy, child birth**, and genetic testing are admissible as evidence without requiring third-party foundation testimony, and shall constitute prima facie evidence of amounts incurred for such services or for genetic testing on behalf of the child.

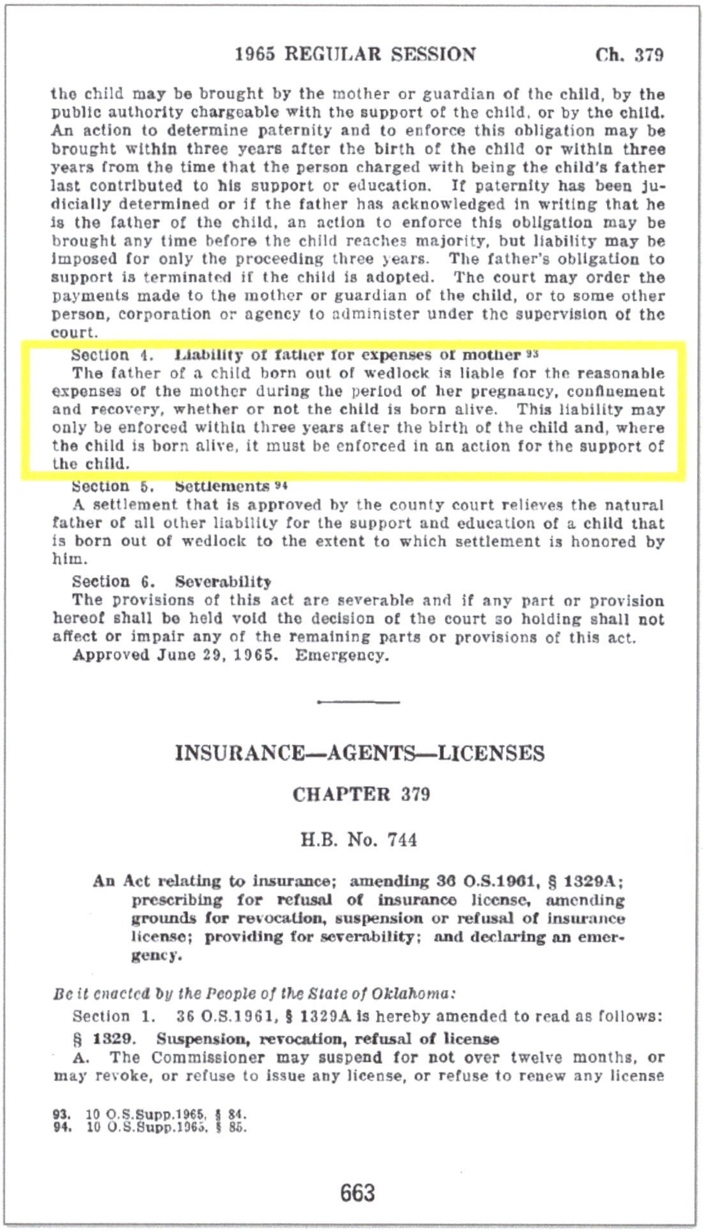
1965 REGULAR SESSION Ch. 379

the child may be brought by the mother or guardian of the child, by the public authority chargeable with the support of the child, or by the child. An action to determine paternity and to enforce this obligation may be brought within three years after the birth of the child or within three years from the time that the person charged with being the child's father last contributed to his support or education. If paternity has been judicially determined or if the father has acknowledged in writing that he is the father of the child, an action to enforce this obligation may be brought any time before the child reaches majority, but liability may be imposed for only the proceeding three years. The father's obligation to support is terminated if the child is adopted. The court may order the payments made to the mother or guardian of the child, or to some other person, corporation or agency to administer under the supervision of the court.

Section 4. **Liability of father for expenses of mother** [93]

The father of a child born out of wedlock is liable for the reasonable expenses of the mother during the period of her pregnancy, confinement and recovery, whether or not the child is born alive. This liability may only be enforced within three years after the birth of the child and, where the child is born alive, it must be enforced in an action for the support of the child.

Section 5. **Settlements** [94]

A settlement that is approved by the county court relieves the natural father of all other liability for the support and education of a child that is born out of wedlock to the extent to which settlement is honored by him.

Section 6. **Severability**

The provisions of this act are severable and if any part or provision hereof shall be held void the decision of the court so holding shall not affect or impair any of the remaining parts or provisions of this act.

Approved June 29, 1965. Emergency.

INSURANCE—AGENTS—LICENSES

CHAPTER 379

H.B. No. 744

An Act relating to insurance; amending 36 O.S.1961, § 1329A; prescribing for refusal of insurance license, amending grounds for revocation, suspension or refusal of insurance license; providing for severability; and declaring an emergency.

Be it enacted by the People of the State of Oklahoma:

Section 1. 36 O.S.1961, § 1329A is hereby amended to read as follows:

§ 1329. **Suspension, revocation, refusal of license**

A. The Commissioner may suspend for not over twelve months, or may revoke, or refuse to issue any license, or refuse to renew any license

93. 10 O.S.Supp.1965, § 84.
94. 10 O.S.Supp.1965, § 85.

663

Figure 50: *Laws*, ch.378 (Okla., 1965)

Oregon

General Laws, Title XXI, §2554 *(Duties and Obligations; Laws 1917 ch.48 §5)*

Upon the trial of the case the issue shall be as to whether the accused is guilty or not guilty; and if the mother of the child be dead, her examination taken before the justice may be read in evidence, and in all cases it shall be read when demanded by the accused. If the accused shall be found guilty or shall admit the guilt of the accusation, he shall be adjudged to be the father of such child, and shall stand chargeable with its future maintenance in such sum and in such manner as the court shall direct, and also for **all expenses incurred by such county or by the mother of such child for the lying-in and attendance of the mother during her sickness**, and also for the care and support of such child since its birth, and for the costs of the prosecution. All which matters shall be ascertained and fixed by the court, and shall be inserted in the judgment; provided, however, that the judgment of the court providing for the maintenance of such child by the father shall be in a yearly sum not less than $100 nor more than $350 for the first two years, and not less than $150 nor more than $500 for each year succeeding until the child reaches the age of fourteen years; provided further, that defendant shall be entitled to the right of trial by jury, and appeal, as provided in civil actions; and provided further that no conviction shall be had upon the uncorroborated testimony of said female.

Oregon Revised Statutes §109.098(1) *(Objection of putative father...; SL 1975 ch.640, SL 1995 ch.90)*

If a putative father of a child by due appearance in a proceeding of which he is entitled to notice under ORS 109.096 objects to the relief sought, the court:... (b) Shall, if filiation proceedings are not pending, inquire as to the paternity of the child, the putative father's past endeavors to fulfill his obligation to support the child and to contribute to the **pregnancy-related medical expenses**, the period that the child has lived with the putative father, the putative father's fitness to care for and rear the child and whether the putative father is willing to be declared the father of the child and to assume the responsibilities of a father.

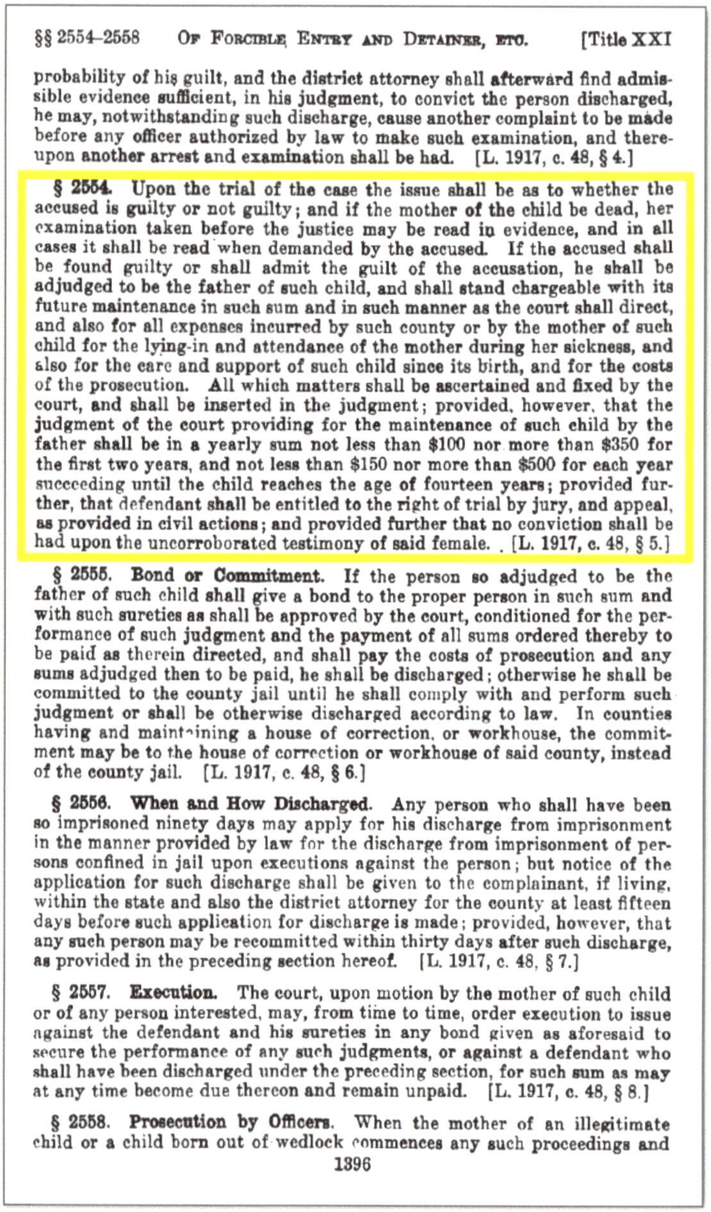

§§ 2554–2558 OF FORCIBLE ENTRY AND DETAINER, ETC. [Title XXI

probability of his guilt, and the district attorney shall afterward find admissible evidence sufficient, in his judgment, to convict the person discharged, he may, notwithstanding such discharge, cause another complaint to be made before any officer authorized by law to make such examination, and thereupon another arrest and examination shall be had. [L. 1917, c. 48, § 4.]

§ 2554. Upon the trial of the case the issue shall be as to whether the accused is guilty or not guilty; and if the mother of the child be dead, her examination taken before the justice may be read in evidence, and in all cases it shall be read when demanded by the accused. If the accused shall be found guilty or shall admit the guilt of the accusation, he shall be adjudged to be the father of such child, and shall stand chargeable with its future maintenance in such sum and in such manner as the court shall direct, and also for all expenses incurred by such county or by the mother of such child for the lying-in and attendance of the mother during her sickness, and also for the care and support of such child since its birth, and for the costs of the prosecution. All which matters shall be ascertained and fixed by the court, and shall be inserted in the judgment; provided, however, that the judgment of the court providing for the maintenance of such child by the father shall be in a yearly sum not less than $100 nor more than $350 for the first two years, and not less than $150 nor more than $500 for each year succeeding until the child reaches the age of fourteen years; provided further, that defendant shall be entitled to the right of trial by jury, and appeal, as provided in civil actions; and provided further that no conviction shall be had upon the uncorroborated testimony of said female. [L. 1917, c. 48, § 5.]

§ 2555. Bond or Commitment. If the person so adjudged to be the father of such child shall give a bond to the proper person in such sum and with such sureties as shall be approved by the court, conditioned for the performance of such judgment and the payment of all sums ordered thereby to be paid as therein directed, and shall pay the costs of prosecution and any sums adjudged then to be paid, he shall be discharged; otherwise he shall be committed to the county jail until he shall comply with and perform such judgment or shall be otherwise discharged according to law. In counties having and maintaining a house of correction, or workhouse, the commitment may be to the house of correction or workhouse of said county, instead of the county jail. [L. 1917, c. 48, § 6.]

§ 2556. When and How Discharged. Any person who shall have been so imprisoned ninety days may apply for his discharge from imprisonment in the manner provided by law for the discharge from imprisonment of persons confined in jail upon executions against the person; but notice of the application for such discharge shall be given to the complainant, if living, within the state and also the district attorney for the county at least fifteen days before such application for discharge is made; provided, however, that any such person may be recommitted within thirty days after such discharge, as provided in the preceding section hereof. [L. 1917, c. 48, § 7.]

§ 2557. Execution. The court, upon motion by the mother of such child or of any person interested, may, from time to time, order execution to issue against the defendant and his sureties in any bond given as aforesaid to secure the performance of any such judgments, or against a defendant who shall have been discharged under the preceding section, for such sum as may at any time become due thereon and remain unpaid. [L. 1917, c. 48, § 8.]

§ 2558. Prosecution by Officers. When the mother of an illegitimate child or a child born out of wedlock commences any such proceedings and

1396

Figure 51: *Laws*, ch.48 (Ore., 1917)

Pennsylvania

Pennsylvania has an ambiguous beginning to prenatal child support. The first codified instance even marginally applicable comes in the 1860 consolidation of the *Penal Laws*. This "Fornication and Bastardy" law added "expenses incurred at the birth of the child" after multiple generations of amendments to the original 1705 *General Laws* section regarding "Adultery and Fornication." That section included penalties of corporal punishment, imprisonment, hard labor, and fines. The convicted father additionally had to pay into the community fund that supported children of the poor.

In 1810 came the first volume of *Smith's Laws*[30], a collection of annotations for Pennsylvania laws. Pages 27-29 analyzed the 1705 laws and their many amendments over the next century. In the final paragraph, there is a brief note stating, "On a conviction of bastardy, the uniform practice has been, to make an allowance for lying-in expenses, and a gross sum for the support of the child from its birth to the time of judgment." It ends with the citation "MSS. Reports, Sup. Court." Thus, sometime between 1705 and 1810, the practice arose within the court system to include pregnancy-related expenses in the requirements. A search through court records turned up Goddard v. the Commonwealth in 1820, which required the defendant to "pay $20 for lying-in expenses" among a list of other fees. Several other cases in the 1820s — including those at the state Supreme Court — affirmed similar penalties.

Figure 52: *Smith's Laws* (1810)

Penal Laws of 1860 (Fornication and Bastardy; Laws 1860 ch. 374 sec. 38, amended from Laws 1705 ch. CXXII)

...; and such person being thereof convicted, shall be sentenced, in addition to the fine aforesaid, to **pay the expenses incurred at the birth of such child**, and to give security, by one or more sureties, and in such sum as the court shall direct, to the guardians, directors or overseers of the poor of the city, county or township where such child was born, to perform such order for the maintenance of the said child, as the court before which such conviction is had shall direct and appoint.

Figure 53: *Laws*, ch.374 (Penn., 1860)

Pennsylvania Consolidated Statutes §23-4326(l) *(Mandatory inclusion of child medical support; Act 58, 1997)*

"Birth-related expenses." **Costs of reasonable and necessary health care for the mother or child or both incurred before, during or after the birth of a child born in or out of wedlock which are the result of the pregnancy or birth and which benefit either the mother or child**. Charges not related to the pregnancy or birth shall be excluded.

Pennsylvania Consolidated Statutes §23-4343(a) *(Paternity; Act 58, 1997)*

Where the paternity of a child born out of wedlock is disputed, the determination of paternity shall be made by the court in a civil action without a jury. A putative father may not be prohibited from initiating a civil action to establish paternity. The burden of proof shall be by a preponderance of the evidence. **Bills for pregnancy, childbirth, postnatal care related to the pregnancy** and genetic testing are admissible as evidence without requiring third-party foundation testimony and shall constitute prima facie evidence of amounts incurred for such services or for testing on behalf of the child. If there is clear and convincing evidence of paternity on the basis of genetic tests or other evidence, the court shall upon motion of a party issue a temporary order of support pending the judicial resolution of a dispute regarding paternity. The Supreme Court shall provide by general rule for entry of a default order establishing paternity upon a showing of service of process on the defendant and a subsequent failure to appear for scheduled genetic testing.

Rhode Island

11 General Laws §73-4 *(Maintenance of bastard children; PL 1873 ch.288)*
...or he may plead guilty or nolo contendere before said justice court, in which case said justice court shall adjudge him the putative father of said child, and shall order him to pay to said overseer of the poor, by installments or otherwise, such sum as may, in the judgment of said court, be necessary to **defray the expenses of the lying-in of such woman** and the support of said child, and of the other expenses of said town in connection with said complaint, and the costs of said complaint...

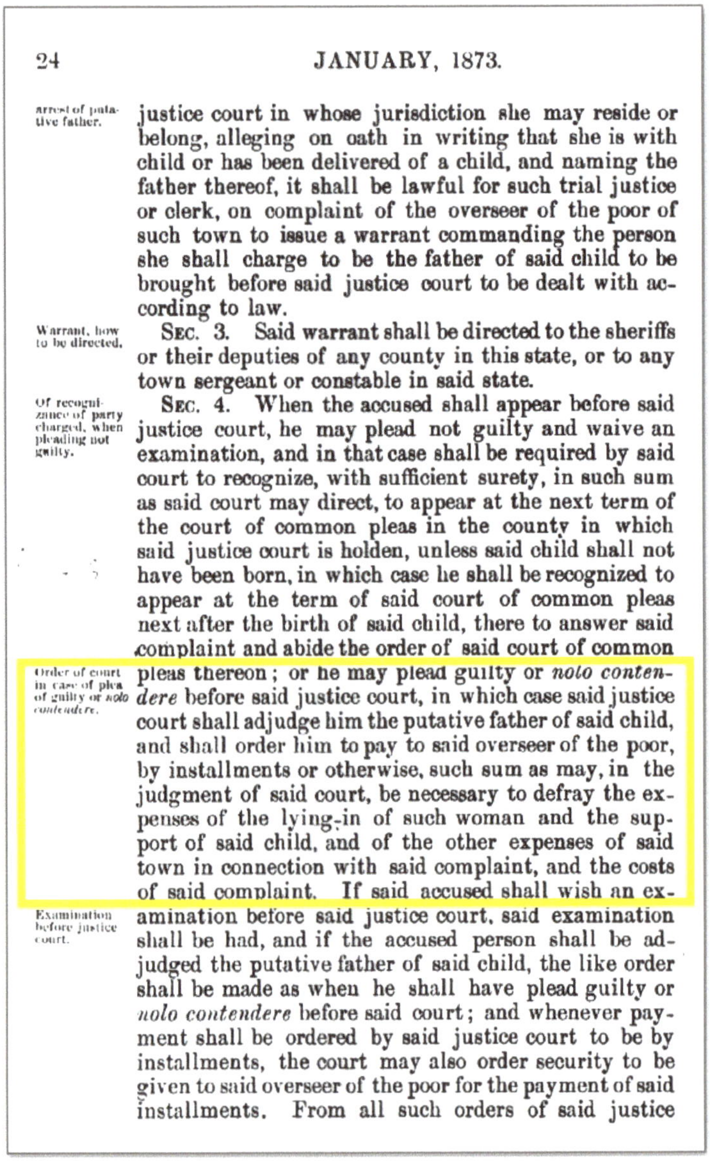

24 JANUARY, 1873.

arrest of putative father.

justice court in whose jurisdiction she may reside or belong, alleging on oath in writing that she is with child or has been delivered of a child, and naming the father thereof, it shall be lawful for such trial justice or clerk, on complaint of the overseer of the poor of such town to issue a warrant commanding the person she shall charge to be the father of said child to be brought before said justice court to be dealt with according to law.

Warrant, how to be directed.

SEC. 3. Said warrant shall be directed to the sheriffs or their deputies of any county in this state, or to any town sergeant or constable in said state.

Of recognizance of party charged, when pleading not guilty.

SEC. 4. When the accused shall appear before said justice court, he may plead not guilty and waive an examination, and in that case shall be required by said court to recognize, with sufficient surety, in such sum as said court may direct, to appear at the next term of the court of common pleas in the county in which said justice court is holden, unless said child shall not have been born, in which case he shall be recognized to appear at the term of said court of common pleas next after the birth of said child, there to answer said complaint and abide the order of said court of common pleas thereon; or he may plead guilty or *nolo contendere* before said justice court, in which case said justice court shall adjudge him the putative father of said child, and shall order him to pay to said overseer of the poor, by installments or otherwise, such sum as may, in the judgment of said court, be necessary to defray the expenses of the lying-in of such woman and the support of said child, and of the other expenses of said town in connection with said complaint, and the costs of said complaint. If said accused shall wish an examination before said justice court, said examination shall be had, and if the accused person shall be adjudged the putative father of said child, the like order shall be made as when he shall have plead guilty or *nolo contendere* before said court; and whenever payment shall be ordered by said justice court to be by installments, the court may also order security to be given to said overseer of the poor for the payment of said installments. From all such orders of said justice

Order of court in case of plea of guilty or nolo contendere.

Examination before justice court.

Figure 54: *Public Laws*, ch.288 (RI, 1873)

General Laws §15-8-1 *(Obligations of the father; PL 1979 ch.185)*
The father of a child which is or may be born out of lawful wedlock is liable to the same extent as the father of a child born in lawful wedlock, whether or not the child is born alive, for the **reasonable expense of the mother's pregnancy and confinement**, and the education, necessary support and maintenance, and medical and funeral expenses of the child and for reasonable counsel fees for the prosecution of paternity proceedings. A child born out of lawful wedlock also includes a child born to a married woman by a man other than her lawful husband.

General Laws §15-8-2 *(Enforcement; PL 1979 ch.185)*
Paternity may be determined upon the complaint of the father, mother, the child, or the public authority chargeable by law with the support of the child. If paternity has been determined or has been acknowledged according to the laws of Rhode Island, the liabilities of the father may be enforced in the same or other proceedings by the mother, the child, or the public authority which has furnished or may furnish the **reasonable expenses of pregnancy, confinement**, education, necessary support, or funeral expenses, and by other persons, including private agencies, to the extent that they have furnished the reasonable expenses of pregnancy, confinement, education, necessary maintenance and support, or funeral expenses.

General Laws §15-8-18(c) *(Judgments; PL 1979 ch.185)*
The judgment or order may contain any other provision directed against the appropriate party to the proceeding, concerning the duty of support, the custody and guardianship of the child, visitation privileges with the child, or any other matter in the best interest of the child. The judgment or order may direct the father to pay the **reasonable expenses of the mother's pregnancy and confinement**.

South Carolina

South Carolina is interesting in that the earliest references to prenatal child support come in identical "statutes at large" for both 1944 and 1954. These acts declare powers of the Domestic Relations Court to include enforcement for "expenses of confinement."

Statutes at Large *(In the exercise of its jurisdiction the court shall have power; Act 1944 No. 509 §43(2), repeated in Act 1954 No. 575 §22(2))*
1. To order support of a wife or child or stepchild or both, irrespective whether they are likely to become a public charge.
2. To include the requirements of an order for support the providing necessary shelter, food, clothing, care, medical attention, **expenses of confinement**, the expense of the education of the child, the payment of funeral expenses, and other proper and reasonable expenses.

Code of Laws §20-7-420(15) *(Jurisdiction of family court in domestic matters; Act 1981 No. 71, repealed in Act 2008 No. 361)*
~~To include in the requirements of an order for support the providing of necessary shelter, food, clothing, care, medical attention, **expenses of confinement, both before and after the birth**, the expense of educating his or her child and other proper and reasonable expenses.~~

No. 509] OF SOUTH CAROLINA 1399

judge to visit each institution to which a delinquent child shall have been committed by the court during the year."

"**SECTION 40: Concurrent jurisdiction with certain courts as to delinquent or neglected children—reformatories.**—Th court shall have all the duties, power, authority and jurisdiction now vested by law in the probate judge of the county, in respect of delinquent or neglected children, which shall be concurrent with that of the probate judge, the circuit court and any special courts of said county, and said courts are hereby authorized to refer any case brought before it to this court. Such jurisdiction shall include the power to commit to the reformatories of the State in proper cases.

SECTION 41: Care and custody of children.—This article shall be construed to the end that the care, custody and discipline of the children brought before the court shall approximate as nearly as possible that which they should receive from their parents, and that as far as practicable they shall be treated not as criminals but as children in need of aid, encouragement and guidance."

SECTION 42: Family court—jurisdiction.—The family court shall have jurisdiction within the county to hear and determine all proceedings to compel the support of a wife, or child, or step-child; and

(2) in proceedings properly brought before the court for the support of a wife, or child, or step-child it shall have jurisdiction for the protection, guardianship and disposition of neglected or dependent minors.

(3) Jurisdiction within the county in all cases or proceedings against persons charged with failure to obey an order of the court made pursuant to authority conferred by law.

SECTION 43: Powers.—In the exercise of its jurisdiction the court shall have power (1) to order support of a wife or child or step-child or both, irrespective of whether they are likely to become a public charge.

(2) To include in the requirements of an order for support the providing of necessary shelter, food, clothing, care, medical attention, expenses of confinement, the expense of educating his child, the payment of funeral expenses, and other proper and reasonable expenses.

(3) To require of persons legally chargeable with the support of a wife, or child, or step-child and who are possessed of sufficient

Figure 55: *Acts*, No. 509 (SC, 1944)

1458 STATUTES AT LARGE [No. 575]
GENERAL AND PERMANENT LAWS—1954

vided by law where jurisdiction is laid in said circuit court. The proceedings shall follow those of the circuit court except that appeals shall be in the first instance to the court of common pleas of the county.

SECTION 21. Same—further jurisdiction.—(a) The Domestic Relations Court shall have jurisdiction within the county to hear and determine all proceedings to compel the support of a wife, or child, or stepchild.

(b) In proceedings properly brought before the court for the support of a wife, or child, or stepchild it shall have jurisdiction for the protection, guardianship and disposition of neglected or dependent minors.

(c) Jurisdiction within the county in all cases or proceedings against persons charged with failure to obey an order of the court made pursuant to authority conferred by law.

SECTION 22. Same—powers.—In the exercise of its jurisdiction the court shall have power:

1. To order support of a wife or child or stepchild or both, irrespective of whether they are likely to become a public charge.
2. To include in the requirements of an order for support the providing of necessary shelter, food, clothing, care, medical attention, expenses of confinement, the expense of the education of the child, the payment of funeral expenses, and other proper and reasonable expenses.
3. To require of persons legally chargeable with the support of a wife, or child, and who are possessed of sufficient means or who are able to earn such means, the payment weekly, or at other fixed periods, of a fair and reasonable sum for such support, or as a contribution toward such support, according to the means of the person so chargeable.
4. To make all orders for support run until further order of the court, except that orders for support of a child shall run until the child is twenty-one years of age; or, where there are physical or mental disabilities of the child or other exceptional circumstances that warrant it, in the discretion of the court during any period and beyond the child's minority as such physical or mental disabilities may continue.
5. To require the support of a wife who needs support where there are no children, even though there is no physical or mental disability.

Figure 56: *Acts*, No. 575 (SC, 1954)

Code of Laws § 63-17-3010(A)(4) *(Personal jurisdiction of nonresident; Act 2008 No. 361)*
the individual resided in this State and provided **prenatal expenses** or support for the child;

Code of Laws § 63-17-3360(D) *(Nonresident party proceedings; Act 2008 No. 361)*
Copies of bills for testing for parentage of a child, and for **prenatal and postnatal health care of the mother and child**, furnished to the adverse party at least ten days before trial, are admissible in evidence to prove the amount of the charges billed and that the charges were reasonable, necessary, and customary.

South Dakota

South Dakota's earliest applicable legislation came twenty-seven years before statehood, under the initial session of the Territory of Dakota in 1862. This statute would held remained active at least until South Dakota and North Dakota became states in 1889. It is unclear if the territorial statutes transferred to statehood or not. As a state, the first law came in 1923 — in the multi-state push for the *Uniform Illegitimacy Act* — and has seen numerous revisions since then.

General Laws and Memorials and Resolutions of the Territory of Dakota, ch. 6, §3 (1862)
If such accused person shall pay or secure to be may be paid to the female complaining, such sum or sums of money, or other property, as she may agree to receive in full satisfaction, and as shall be approved by the commissioners of the county, of which agreement and approval the justice shall make a memorandum upon his docket; and if the accused shall also enter into bonds, with sufficient sureties, to be approved by the justice, to the commissioners of the county in which such female shall reside, and their successors in office, conditioned to secure and indemnify such county from all charges for the maintenance of such child, **and shall also pay expenses, any, incurred such county, for the lying-in, and support and attendance upon the mother such child during her sickness**, and the costs prosecution; then the justice shall discharge such accused person.

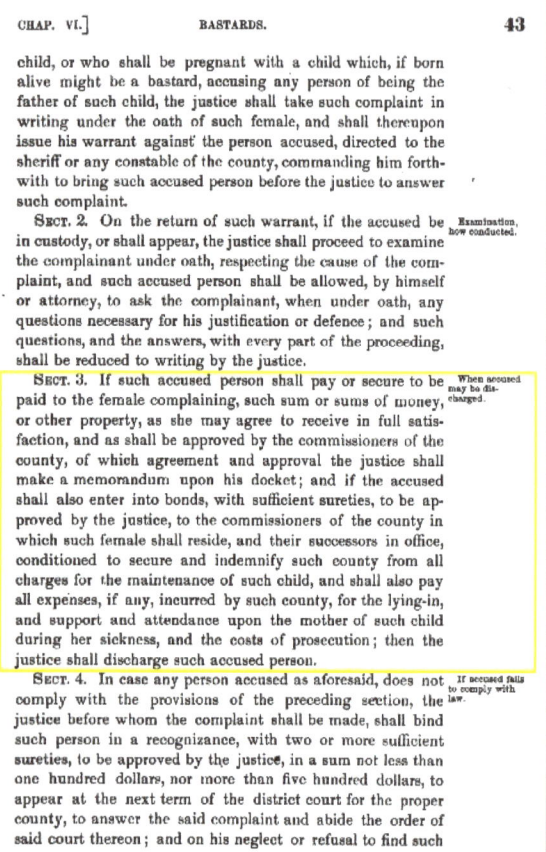

Figure 57: *Session Laws,* ch. 6 (Dakota Terr, 1862)

South Dakota Codified Laws § 25-8-3 (*Uniform Illegitimacy Act, Obligation of parents;* SL 1923 ch.295; codified in South Dakota Code of 1939, vol.2, p.599 as § 37.2101; renumbered in SL 1984, ch 190, § 3, HB 1043)
The father and mother of a child born out of wedlock are jointly and severally liable to pay the **expenses of the mother's pregnancy and confinement**.

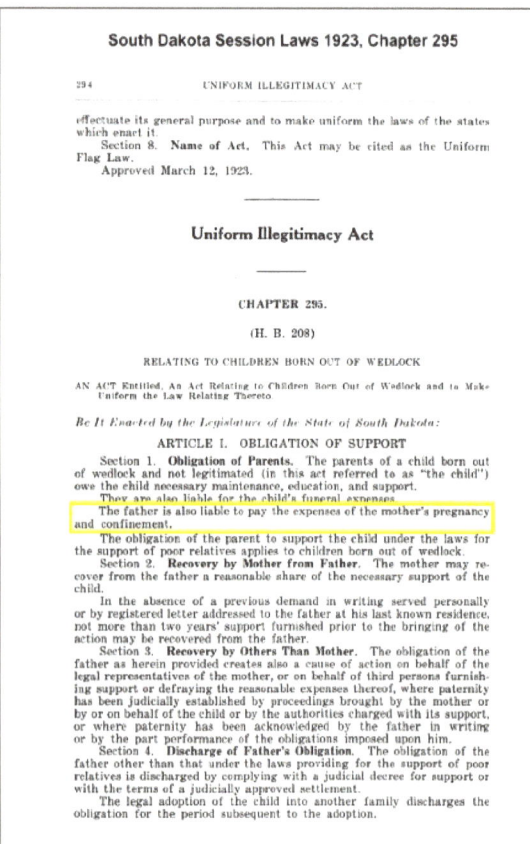

Figure 58: *Session Laws,* ch. 295 (SD, 1923)

Tennessee

Tennessee Code Annotated § 36-2-308(d) *(Order of parentage; Acts 1997 ch.477 as 36-2-108, renumbered in a later session)*
Bills for the mother's care during pregnancy and childbirth and genetic testing shall be admissible without requiring third party foundation testimony and shall constitute prima facie evidence of amounts incurred for such services or for testing on behalf of the child.

Tennessee Code Annotated § 36-2-311(a) *(Order of parentage; Acts 1997 ch.477 as 36-2-111, renumbered in a later session)*
Upon establishing parentage, the court shall make an order declaring the father of the child. This order shall include the following: ... (13) Determination of liability for a mother's **reasonable expenses for her pregnancy, confinement and recovery** to either or both parties

(4) the home telephone number of the mother and the father, if known;

(5) the driver's license numbers of mother and father, if known;

(6) the name, address and telephone number of mother and father's employers, if known;

(7) the availability of health insurance to cover the child, if known;

(8) determination of the child's name on his or her birth certificate;

(9) determination of the custody of the child pursuant to Tennessee Code Annotated, Section 36-6-101 et seq.

(10) determination of visitation or parental access pursuant to Tennessee Code Annotated, Section 36-6-101 et seq.;

(11) determination of child support pursuant to Tennessee Code Annotated, Section 36-5-101 et seq.

In determining retroactive support, if any, deviation from the guidelines may occur at the discretion of the court. The court must make a written finding that application and guidelines would be unjust or inappropriate in order to provide for the best interests of the child or the equity between the parties. Nothing in this provision shall limit the right of the State of Tennessee to recover expenditures made by the State for the benefit of the child or the obligation of the Title IV agency to pursue retroactive support for the custodial parent where appropriate.

(12) determination of liability for funeral expense to either or both parties, if the child is deceased;

(13) determination of liability for a mother's reasonable expenses for her pregnancy, confinement and recovery to either or both parties; and

(14) determination of the liability for counsel fees to either or both parties after consideration of all relevant factors.

Figure 59: *Acts*, ch.477 (Tenn., 1997)

Texas

In 1974, the *Texas Legislature* amended § 15.02 of the *Texas Family Code*, in regards to "involuntary termination of parental rights," to list abandonment and non-support during pregnancy as possible grounds for such termination[31]. It wasn't for another thirteen years that the *Texas Family Code* explicitly required prenatal child support.

Texas Family Code § 13.42(a) *(Conservatorship, Support, Fees, and Payments; Acts 1987 ch.689 § 11)*
In a suit in which a determination of paternity is sought, the court may provide for the managing and possessory conservatorship and support of and access to the child; except that no alleged father denying paternity may be required to make any payment for the support of the child until paternity is established. On a finding of paternity, the court may order support retroactive to the time of the filing of the suit and, on a proper showing, **may order a party to pay an equitable portion of all prenatal and postnatal related health care expenses of the mother and child**.

Texas Family Code § 13.06(f) *(Evidence at Trial; Acts 1989 ch.375 § 17)*
If a copy is provided to the adverse party and to the court at the pretrial conference, submission of a **copy of a medical bill for the prenatal and postnatal health care expenses** of the mother and child or for charges directly related to the paternity testing constitutes a prima facie showing that the charges are reasonable, necessary, and customary and may be admitted as evidence of the truth of the matters stated therein.

[Texas Family Code § 102.011(b)](#) *(Child Support;* [Acts 1995 ch. 20; HB655](#)*)*
The court may also exercise personal jurisdiction over a person on whom service of citation is required or over the person's personal representative, although the person is not a resident or domiciliary of this state, if: (5) the person resided in this state and provided **prenatal expenses** or support for the child;

[Texas Family Code § 159.201(a)](#) *(Base for Jurisdiction over nonresident;* [Acts 1995 ch. 20; HB655](#)*)*
In a proceeding to establish or enforce a support order or to determine parentage of a child, a tribunal of this state may exercise personal jurisdiction over a nonresident individual or the individual's guardian or conservator if: (4) the individual resided in this state and provided **prenatal expenses** or support for the child;

Figure 60: *Acts*, ch.689 sec. 11 (Texas, 1987)

[Texas Family Code § 159.316(d)](#) *(Special rules of evidence and procedure;* [Acts 1995 ch. 20; HB655](#)*)*
Copies of bills for testing for parentage of a child, and for **prenatal and postnatal health care of the mother and child** furnished to the adverse party at least 10 days before trial are admissible in evidence to prove the amount of the charges billed and that the charges were reasonable, necessary, and customary.

[Texas Family Code § 160.621(d)](#) *(Admissibility of results of genetic testing;* [Acts 2001 ch. 821](#)*)*
Copies of bills for genetic testing and for **prenatal and postnatal health care for the mother and child** that are furnished to the adverse party on or before the 10th day before the date of a hearing are admissible to establish:
(1) the amount of the charges billed; and
(2) that the charges were reasonable, necessary, and customary.

[Texas Family Code § 160.636(g)](#) *(Order adjudicating parentage;* [Acts 2001 ch. 821](#)*)*
On a finding of parentage, the court may order retroactive child support as provided by Chapter 154 and, on a proper showing, order a party to pay **an equitable portion of all of the prenatal and postnatal health care expenses of the mother and the child**.

Utah

New to the third edition of this book is Utah's House Bill 113, which was ratified on March 16, 2021. This legislation added a section in the Utah Code to require the father to pay fifty percent of all prenatal expenses, including health insurance premiums.

Utah Code § 78B-14-201 (Jurisdiction over nonresident; Laws 1996 Ch. 149 § 6 as 77-31a-201; renumbered in Laws 1997 Ch. 232 § 111 to 78-45f-201; renumbered in Laws 2008 Ch. 3 § 1433, HB78)
In a proceeding to establish, enforce, or modify a support order or to determine parentage, a tribunal of this state may exercise personal jurisdiction over a nonresident individual, or the individual's guardian or conservator, if: ... (4) the individual resided in this state and **provided prenatal expenses** or support for the child

Utah Code § 78B-14-316(4) (Special rules of evidence and procedure; Laws 1997 Ch. 232 § 111 as 78-45f-316; renumbered in Laws 2015 Ch. 45, SB191)
Copies of bills for testing for parentage of a child, and for **prenatal and postnatal health care of the mother and child**, furnished to the adverse party at least 10 days before trial, are admissible in evidence to prove the amount of the charges billed and that the charges were reasonable, necessary, and customary.

Utah Code § 78B-15-613(5) (Admissibility of results of genetic testing; Laws 2005 Ch. 150 § 71 as 78-45g-613; renumbered in Laws 2008 Ch. 3 § 1433, HB78)
Copies of bills for genetic testing and for **prenatal and postnatal health care for the mother and child** which are furnished to the adverse party not less than 10 days before the date of a hearing are admissible to establish:
(a) the amount of charges bills; and
(b) That the charges were reasonable, necessary, and customary.

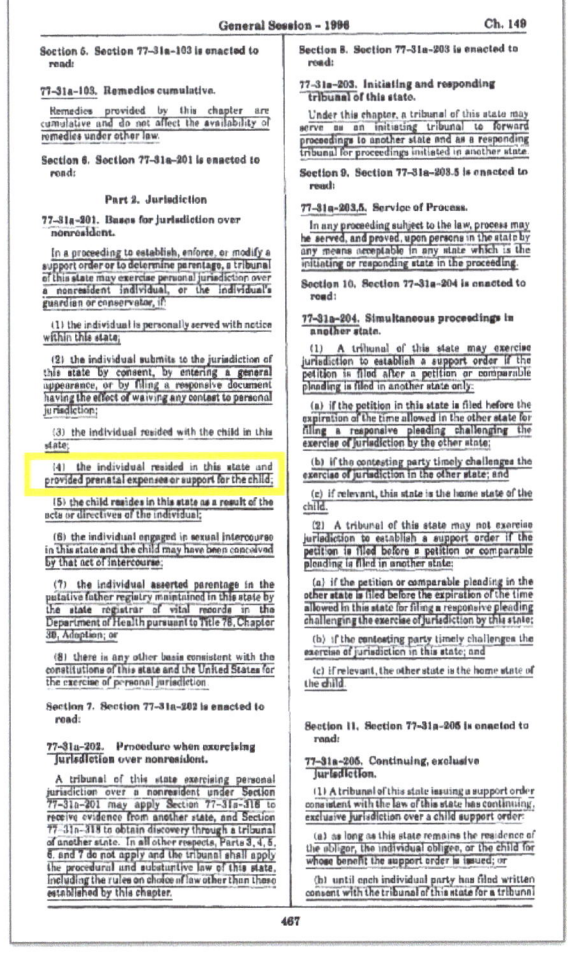

Figure 61: *Laws*, Ch. 149 (Utah, 1996)

Utah Code § 78B-12-105.1 (Duty of biological father to share pregnancy expenses; HB0113, 2021)
(1) Except as otherwise provided in this section, a biological father of a child has a duty to pay 50% of the mother's pregnancy expenses.
(2)
(a) If paternity is disputed, a biological father owes no duty under this section until the biological father's paternity is established.
(b) Once paternity is established, the biological father is subject to Subsection (1).
(3)
(a) Any portion of a mother's pregnancy expenses paid by the mother or the biological father reduces that parent's 50% share under Subsection (1), not the total amount of pregnancy expenses.
(b) Subsection (3)(a) applies regardless of when the mother or biological father pays the pregnancy expense.

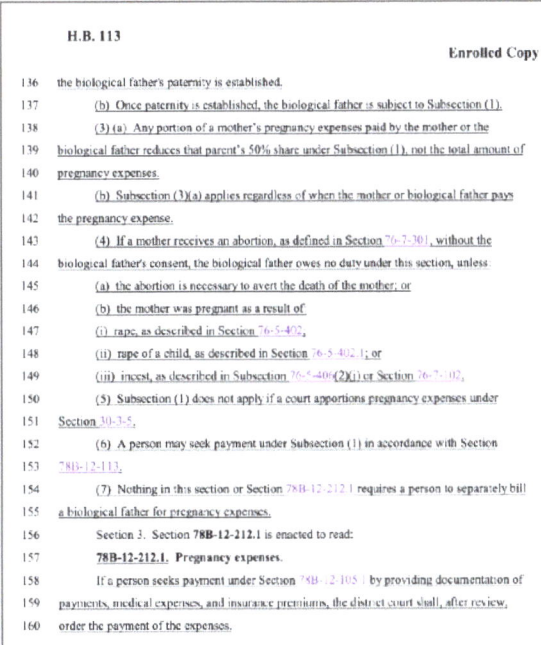

Figure 62: House Bill 113 (Utah, 2021)

Vermont

Vermont was the last state to have a collection of statutes using the now-archaic title "Maintenance of Bastard Children." This entire subchapter of 15 VSA § 331-380 was repealed in 1983 No. 231.

15 Vermont Statutes Annotated, § 304(g) *(Parentage proceedings; 1997 No. 63 § 4, H.208; Repealed in 2017 No 162 § 2, H.562)*
~~Written **bills for pregnancy, childbirth**, and genetic testing costs shall be admissible as evidence without requiring third party foundation testimony, and shall constitute prima facie evidence of amounts incurred for such services or for testing on behalf of the child.~~

15B Vermont Statutes Annotated § 1201(a)(4) *(Bases for jurisdiction over nonresident; 2015 No 16 § 2, H.86)*
The individual resided in this State and provided **prenatal expenses** or support for the child.

15B Vermont Statutes Annotated § 1316(d) *(Bases for jurisdiction over nonresident; 2015 No 16 § 2, H.86)*
Copies of bills for testing for parentage of a child, and for **prenatal and postnatal health care of the mother and child**, furnished to the adverse party at least 10 days before trial, are admissible in evidence to prove the amount of the charges billed and that the charges were reasonable, necessary, and customary.

15C Vermont Statutes Annotated § 616(e) *(Precluding establishment of parentage by perpetrator of sexual assault; 2018 No 162, H.562)*
If the court finds that the burden of proof under subsection (d) of this section is met, the court shall enter an order:
…
(3) requiring that the person alleged to have committed a sexual assault pay child support or **birth-related costs**, or both, unless the person giving birth requests otherwise.

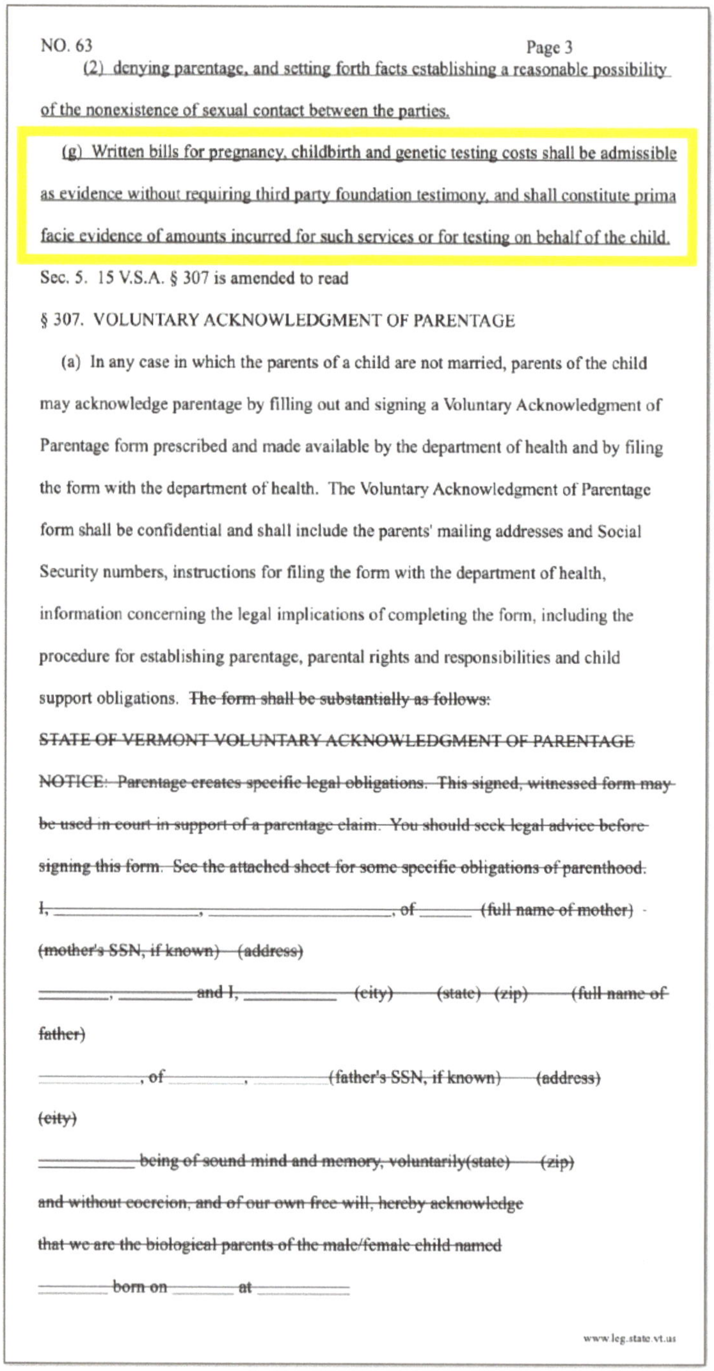
NO. 63 Page 3

(2) denying parentage, and setting forth facts establishing a reasonable possibility of the nonexistence of sexual contact between the parties.

(g) Written bills for pregnancy, childbirth and genetic testing costs shall be admissible as evidence without requiring third party foundation testimony, and shall constitute prima facie evidence of amounts incurred for such services or for testing on behalf of the child.

Sec. 5. 15 V.S.A. § 307 is amended to read

§ 307. VOLUNTARY ACKNOWLEDGMENT OF PARENTAGE

(a) In any case in which the parents of a child are not married, parents of the child may acknowledge parentage by filling out and signing a Voluntary Acknowledgment of Parentage form prescribed and made available by the department of health and by filing the form with the department of health. The Voluntary Acknowledgment of Parentage form shall be confidential and shall include the parents' mailing addresses and Social Security numbers, instructions for filing the form with the department of health, information concerning the legal implications of completing the form, including the procedure for establishing parentage, parental rights and responsibilities and child support obligations. ~~The form shall be substantially as follows:~~

~~STATE OF VERMONT VOLUNTARY ACKNOWLEDGMENT OF PARENTAGE~~

~~NOTICE: Parentage creates specific legal obligations. This signed, witnessed form may be used in court in support of a parentage claim. You should seek legal advice before signing this form. See the attached sheet for some specific obligations of parenthood.~~

~~I, ________, ________, of ______ (full name of mother) (mother's SSN, if known) (address)~~

~~______, ______ and I, ________ (city) (state) (zip) (full name of father)~~

~~______, of ______, ______ (father's SSN, if known) (address) (city)~~

~~______ being of sound mind and memory, voluntarily (state) (zip) and without coercion, and of our own free will, hereby acknowledge that we are the biological parents of the male/female child named ______ born on ______ at ______~~

www.leg.state.vt.us

Figure 63: *Acts*, No. 63 (Vt., 1997)

Virginia

Code of Virginia § 20-49.7 *(Civil actions; Acts 1997 ch.792/ch. 896)*
An action brought under this chapter is a civil action. The natural parent and the alleged parent are competent to testify. Testimony of a physician concerning the medical circumstances of the pregnancy and the condition and characteristics of the child upon birth shall not be privileged. **Bills for expenses incurred for pregnancy, childbirth** and genetic testing shall be admissible as prima facie evidence of the facts stated therein, without requiring third-party foundation testimony if the party offering such evidence is under oath.

Code of Virginia § 20-49.8(A) *(Judgment or order; Acts 1988 ch.878 p1813, S23)*
A judgment or order establishing parentage may include any provision directed against the appropriate party to the proceeding, concerning the duty of support, including an equitable apportionment of the expenses incurred on behalf of the child from the date the proceeding under this chapter was filed with the court against the alleged parent or, if earlier, the date an order of the Department of Social Services entered pursuant to Title 63.2 and directing payment of support was delivered to the sheriff or process server for service upon the obligor. The judgment or order may be in favor of the natural parent or any other person or agency who incurred such expenses provided the complainant exercised due diligence in the service of the respondent. The judgment or order may also include provisions for the custody and guardianship of the child, visitation privileges with the child, or any other matter in the best interest of the child. In circumstances where the parent is outside the jurisdiction of the court, the court may enter a further order requiring the furnishing of bond or other security for the payment required by the judgment or order. **The judgment or order may direct either party to pay the reasonable and necessary unpaid expenses of the mother's pregnancy and delivery** or equitably apportion the unpaid expenses between the parties. However, when the Commonwealth, through the Medicaid program, has paid such expenses, the court may order reimbursement to the Commonwealth for such expenses.

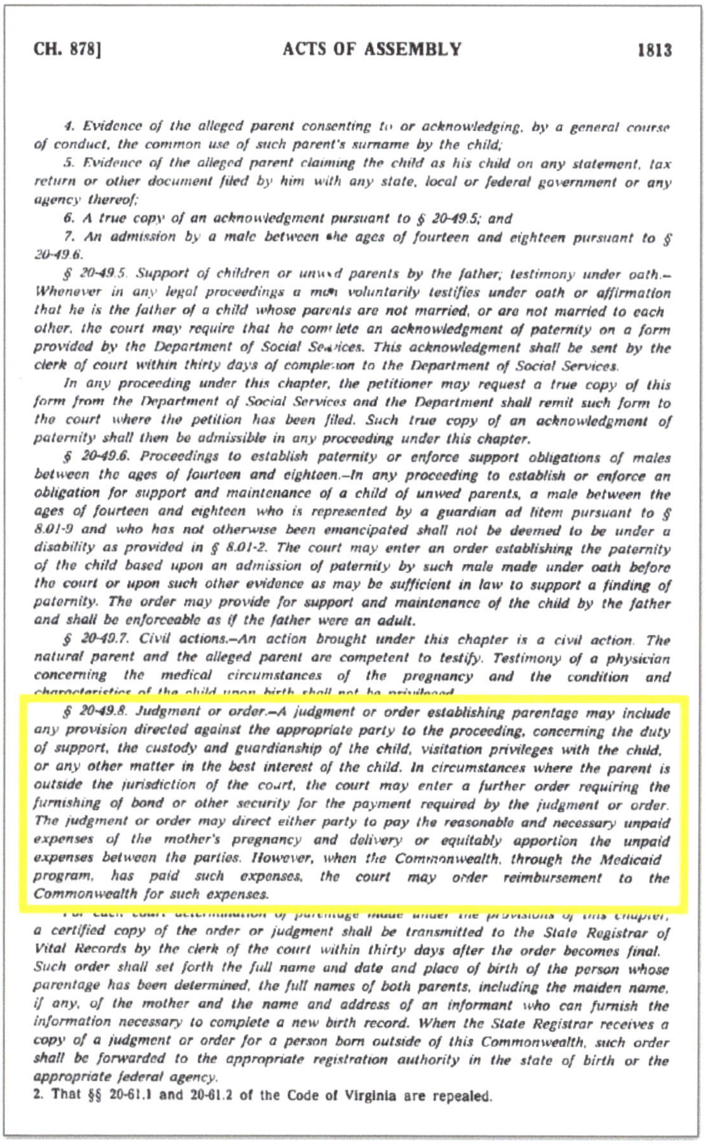

CH. 878] ACTS OF ASSEMBLY 1813

4. Evidence of the alleged parent consenting to or acknowledging, by a general course of conduct, the common use of such parent's surname by the child;

5. Evidence of the alleged parent claiming the child as his child on any statement, tax return or other document filed by him with any state, local or federal government or any agency thereof;

6. A true copy of an acknowledgment pursuant to § 20-49.5; and

7. An admission by a male between the ages of fourteen and eighteen pursuant to § 20-49.6.

§ 20-49.5. Support of children of unwed parents by the father; testimony under oath.–Whenever in any legal proceedings a man voluntarily testifies under oath or affirmation that he is the father of a child whose parents are not married, or are not married to each other, the court may require that he complete an acknowledgment of paternity on a form provided by the Department of Social Services. This acknowledgment shall be sent by the clerk of court within thirty days of completion to the Department of Social Services.

In any proceeding under this chapter, the petitioner may request a true copy of this form from the Department of Social Services and the Department shall remit such form to the court where the petition has been filed. Such true copy of an acknowledgment of paternity shall then be admissible in any proceeding under this chapter.

§ 20-49.6. Proceedings to establish paternity or enforce support obligations of males between the ages of fourteen and eighteen.–In any proceeding to establish or enforce an obligation for support and maintenance of a child of unwed parents, a male between the ages of fourteen and eighteen who is represented by a guardian ad litem pursuant to § 8.01-9 and who has not otherwise been emancipated shall not be deemed to be under a disability as provided in § 8.01-2. The court may enter an order establishing the paternity of the child based upon an admission of paternity by such male made under oath before the court or upon such other evidence as may be sufficient in law to support a finding of paternity. The order may provide for support and maintenance of the child by the father and shall be enforceable as if the father were an adult.

§ 20-49.7. Civil actions.–An action brought under this chapter is a civil action. The natural parent and the alleged parent are competent to testify. Testimony of a physician concerning the medical circumstances of the pregnancy and the condition and characteristics of the child upon birth shall not be privileged.

§ 20-49.8. Judgment or order.–A judgment or order establishing parentage may include any provision directed against the appropriate party to the proceeding, concerning the duty of support, the custody and guardianship of the child, visitation privileges with the child, or any other matter in the best interest of the child. In circumstances where the parent is outside the jurisdiction of the court, the court may enter a further order requiring the furnishing of bond or other security for the payment required by the judgment or order. The judgment or order may direct either party to pay the reasonable and necessary unpaid expenses of the mother's pregnancy and delivery or equitably apportion the unpaid expenses between the parties. However, when the Commonwealth, through the Medicaid program, has paid such expenses, the court may order reimbursement to the Commonwealth for such expenses.

For each court determination of parentage made under the provisions of this chapter, a certified copy of the order or judgment shall be transmitted to the State Registrar of Vital Records by the clerk of the court within thirty days after the order becomes final. Such order shall set forth the full name and date and place of birth of the person whose parentage has been determined, the full names of both parents, including the maiden name, if any, of the mother and the name and address of an informant who can furnish the information necessary to complete a new birth record. When the State Registrar receives a copy of a judgment or order for a person born outside of this Commonwealth, such order shall be forwarded to the appropriate registration authority in the state of birth or the appropriate federal agency.

2. That §§ 20-61.1 and 20-61.2 of the Code of Virginia are repealed.

Figure 64: *Acts*, ch.878 (Va., 1988)

Code of Virginia § 20-108.2(D1) *(Guideline for determination of child support; Acts 2020 ch.177)*
In any initial child support proceeding commenced within six months of the birth of a child, except for good cause shown or the agreement of the parties, in addition to any other child support obligations established pursuant to this section, the child support order shall provide that the parents pay in proportion to their gross incomes, **as used for calculating the monthly support obligation, any reasonable and necessary unpaid expenses of the mother's pregnancy and the delivery of such child**. Any amount paid under this subsection shall not be adjusted by, nor added to, the child support calculated in accordance with subsection G.

Washington

Unknown code section *(Judgment ordering support of child; SL 1919, ch. 203 sec. 9, p.712)*
...he shall be charged by the order and judgment of the court to pay a sum to be therein specified, during each year of the life of such child, until such child shall have reached the age of sixteen years, for the care, education and support of such child, and shall also **be charged thereby to pay the expenses of the mother incurred during her sickness and confinement**, together with all costs of the suit, for which costs execution shall issue as in other cases.

Revised Code of Washington § 26.26B.020(3) *(Support judgment and orders; 1975-'76 2nd ex.s, ch.42)*
The judgment and order shall contain other appropriate provisions directed to the appropriate parties to the proceeding, concerning the duty of current and future support, the extent of any liability for past support furnished to the child if that issue is before the court, the furnishing of bond or other security for the payment of the judgment, or any other matter in the best interest of the child. The judgment and order may direct one parent to pay the **reasonable expenses of the mother's pregnancy and childbirth**. The judgment and order may include a continuing restraining order or injunction. In issuing the order, the court shall consider the provisions of RCW 9.41.800.

Revised Code of Washington § 26.26B.080(1) *(Support judgment and orders; 1975-'76 2nd ex.s ch.42)*
If existence of the parent and child relationship is declared, or parentage or a duty of support has been acknowledged or adjudicated under this chapter or chapter 26.26A RCW or under prior law, the obligation of the parent may be enforced in the same or other proceedings by the other parent, the child, the state of Washington, the public authority that has furnished or may furnish the **reasonable expenses of pregnancy, childbirth**, education, support, or funeral, or by any other person, including a private agency, to the extent he or she has furnished or is furnishing these expenses.

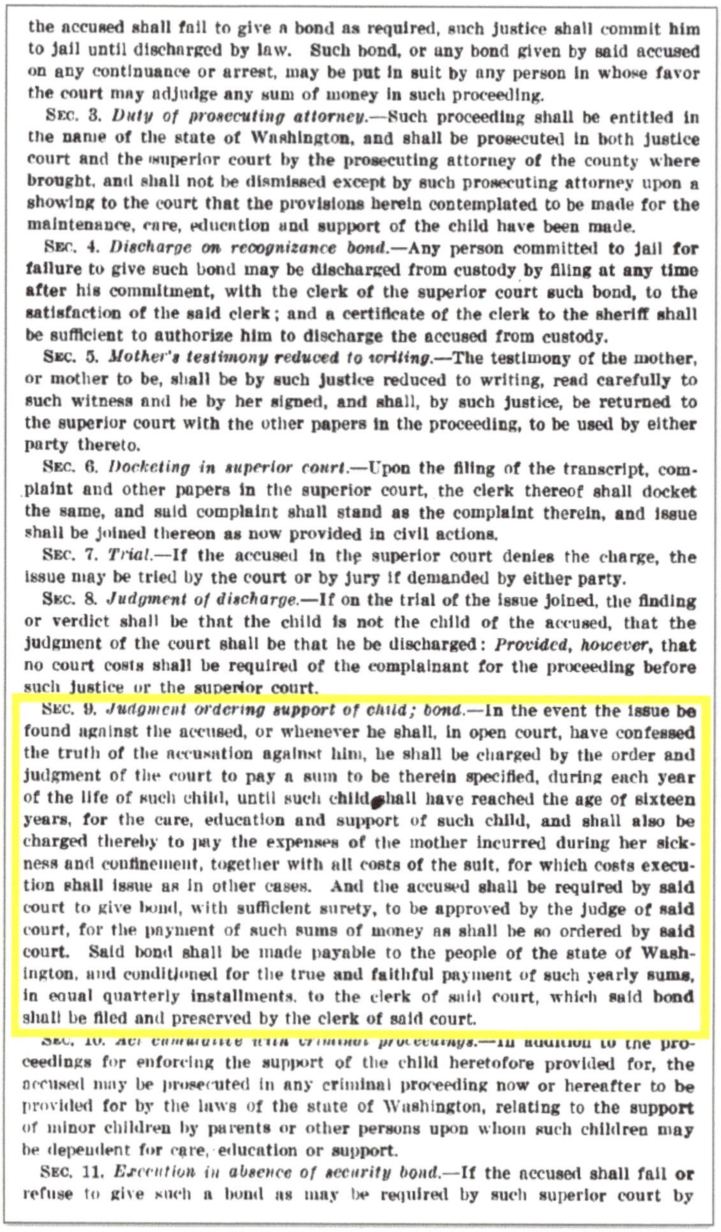

the accused shall fail to give a bond as required, such justice shall commit him to jail until discharged by law. Such bond, or any bond given by said accused on any continuance or arrest, may be put in suit by any person in whose favor the court may adjudge any sum of money in such proceeding.

SEC. 3. *Duty of prosecuting attorney.*—Such proceeding shall be entitled in the name of the state of Washington, and shall be prosecuted in both justice court and the superior court by the prosecuting attorney of the county where brought, and shall not be dismissed except by such prosecuting attorney upon a showing to the court that the provisions herein contemplated to be made for the maintenance, care, education and support of the child have been made.

SEC. 4. *Discharge on recognizance bond.*—Any person committed to jail for failure to give such bond may be discharged from custody by filing at any time after his commitment, with the clerk of the superior court such bond, to the satisfaction of the said clerk; and a certificate of the clerk to the sheriff shall be sufficient to authorize him to discharge the accused from custody.

SEC. 5. *Mother's testimony reduced to writing.*—The testimony of the mother, or mother to be, shall be by such justice reduced to writing, read carefully to such witness and be by her signed, and shall, by such justice, be returned to the superior court with the other papers in the proceeding, to be used by either party thereto.

SEC. 6. *Docketing in superior court.*—Upon the filing of the transcript, complaint and other papers in the superior court, the clerk thereof shall docket the same, and said complaint shall stand as the complaint therein, and issue shall be joined thereon as now provided in civil actions.

SEC. 7. *Trial.*—If the accused in the superior court denies the charge, the issue may be tried by the court or by jury if demanded by either party.

SEC. 8. *Judgment of discharge.*—If on the trial of the issue joined, the finding or verdict shall be that the child is not the child of the accused, that the judgment of the court shall be that he be discharged: *Provided, however*, that no court costs shall be required of the complainant for the proceeding before such justice or the superior court.

SEC. 9. *Judgment ordering support of child; bond.*—In the event the issue be found against the accused, or whenever he shall, in open court, have confessed the truth of the accusation against him, he shall be charged by the order and judgment of the court to pay a sum to be therein specified, during each year of the life of such child, until such child shall have reached the age of sixteen years, for the care, education and support of such child, and shall also be charged thereby to pay the expenses of the mother incurred during her sickness and confinement, together with all costs of the suit, for which costs execution shall issue as in other cases. And the accused shall be required by said court to give bond, with sufficient surety, to be approved by the judge of said court, for the payment of such sums of money as shall be so ordered by said court. Said bond shall be made payable to the people of the state of Washington, and conditioned for the true and faithful payment of such yearly sums, in equal quarterly installments, to the clerk of said court, which said bond shall be filed and preserved by the clerk of said court.

SEC. 10. *Act cumulative with criminal proceedings.*—In addition to the proceedings for enforcing the support of the child heretofore provided for, the accused may be prosecuted in any criminal proceeding now or hereafter to be provided for by the laws of the state of Washington, relating to the support of minor children by parents or other persons upon whom such children may be dependent for care, education or support.

SEC. 11. *Execution in absence of security bond.*—If the accused shall fail or refuse to give such a bond as may be required by such superior court by

Figure 65: *Session Laws*, ch.203 (Wash., 1919)

West Virginia

West Virginia Code, §48-1-244(3) *(Support defined; Acts 1986, ch. 42 as 48A-1-3(20)(C); renumbered in Acts 1996, ch. 110 to 48A-1A-29(C); renumbered in Acts 2001, ch. 91)*
For a mother, ordered by a court of competent jurisdiction, for the **necessary expenses incurred by or for the mother in connection with her confinement or of other expenses in connection with the pregnancy** of the mother.

West Virginia Code, §48-24-104(e) *(Establishment of paternity and duty of support.; Acts 1998 ch. 79 as 48A-6-4(d); renumbered in Acts 2001 ch. 91)*
Bills for pregnancy, childbirth and genetic testing are admissible and constitute prima facie evidence of medical expenses incurred.

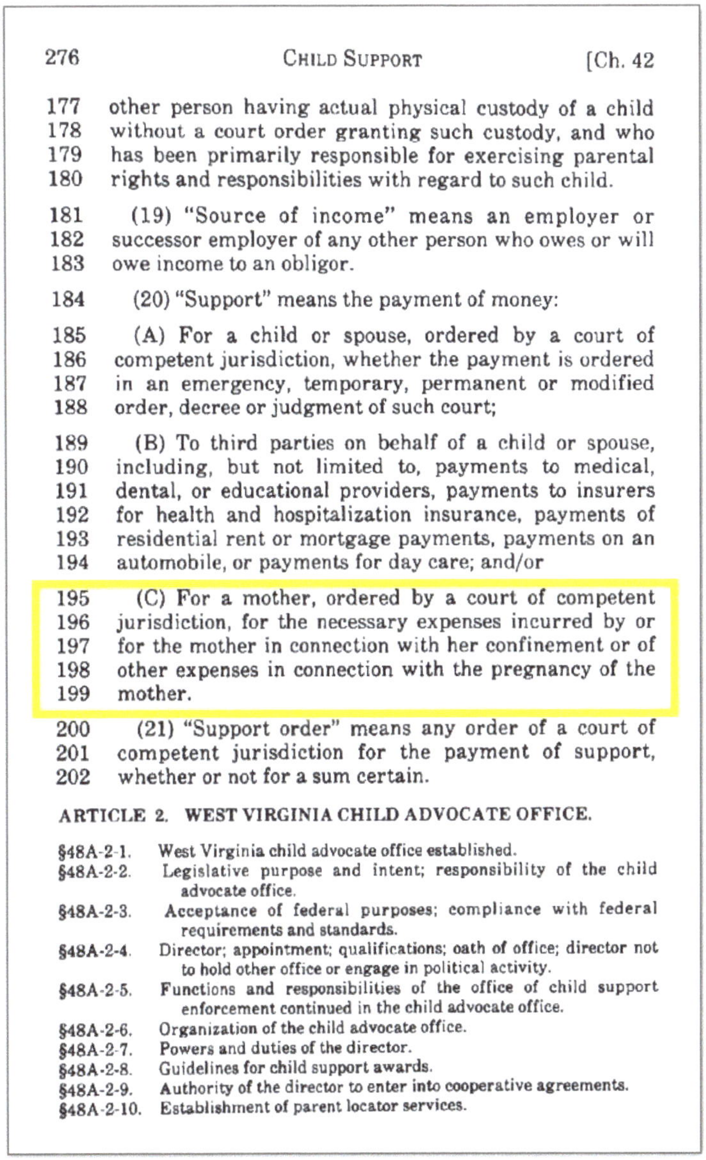
276 CHILD SUPPORT [Ch. 42

other person having actual physical custody of a child without a court order granting such custody, and who has been primarily responsible for exercising parental rights and responsibilities with regard to such child.

(19) "Source of income" means an employer or successor employer of any other person who owes or will owe income to an obligor.

(20) "Support" means the payment of money:

(A) For a child or spouse, ordered by a court of competent jurisdiction, whether the payment is ordered in an emergency, temporary, permanent or modified order, decree or judgment of such court;

(B) To third parties on behalf of a child or spouse, including, but not limited to, payments to medical, dental, or educational providers, payments to insurers for health and hospitalization insurance, payments of residential rent or mortgage payments, payments on an automobile, or payments for day care; and/or

(C) For a mother, ordered by a court of competent jurisdiction, for the necessary expenses incurred by or for the mother in connection with her confinement or of other expenses in connection with the pregnancy of the mother.

(21) "Support order" means any order of a court of competent jurisdiction for the payment of support, whether or not for a sum certain.

ARTICLE 2. WEST VIRGINIA CHILD ADVOCATE OFFICE.

§48A-2-1. West Virginia child advocate office established.
§48A-2-2. Legislative purpose and intent; responsibility of the child advocate office.
§48A-2-3. Acceptance of federal purposes; compliance with federal requirements and standards.
§48A-2-4. Director; appointment; qualifications; oath of office; director not to hold other office or engage in political activity.
§48A-2-5. Functions and responsibilities of the office of child support enforcement continued in the child advocate office.
§48A-2-6. Organization of the child advocate office.
§48A-2-7. Powers and duties of the director.
§48A-2-8. Guidelines for child support awards.
§48A-2-9. Authority of the director to enter into cooperative agreements.
§48A-2-10. Establishment of parent locator services.

Figure 66: *Acts*, ch.42 (WV, 1986)

Wisconsin

Wisconsin's initial prenatal child support requirement came in 1845, under the territorial legislature. The first state legislative session of 1848 directed existing laws to be compiled into the *Revised Statutes of 1849* the following year.

Uncodified Territorial Statutes (For the Support of Illegitimate Children; Acts 1845, p.30, §2)
That whenever any person shall be required to give bail for the maintainance of any child by the provisions of this act or of the act of which this is amendatory, he shall also, at the same time, and in the same bond, be required to **give security for the payment of all costs and expenses incurred for the lying in and the support and attendance upon the mother of such child**, during her sickness; and also for the care and support of such child prior to the giving of such bond.

Revised Statutes of 1849, § 11-31 (Of the Support of Bastards; Acts 1848 ch. 31)
...and if the accused shall also enter into bonds, with sufficient sureties to be approved by the justice, to the supervisors of the town in which such female shall reside, and their successors in office, conditioned to secure and indemnify such town from all charges for the maintenance of such child, and shall also **pay all expenses, if any, incurred by such town for the lying and the support and attendance upon the mother of such child during her sickness**, and the costs of the prosecution, then the justice shall discharge such accused person.

18 Wisconsin Statutes, §767.89(3)(e)(1) *(Paternity judgment; Acts 1979, ch. 352 as 767.51, renumbered in Acts 2005, ch. 443)*
An order establishing the amount of the father's obligation to pay or contribute to the **reasonable expenses of the mother's pregnancy and the child's birth**. The amount established may not exceed one-half of the total actual and reasonable pregnancy and birth expenses. The order also shall specify the court's findings as to whether the father's income is at or below the poverty line established under 42 USC 9902 (2), and shall specify whether periodic payments are due on the obligation, based on the father's ability to pay or contribute to those expenses.

18 Wisconsin Statutes § 767.87(11) *(Testimony and evidence relating to paternity; Acts 1997 ch.191 as 767.47, renumbered in Acts 2005 ch.443)*
RELATED COSTS ADMISSIBLE. **Bills for services or articles related to the pregnancy, childbirth** or genetic testing may be admitted into evidence and are prima facie evidence of the costs incurred for such services or articles.

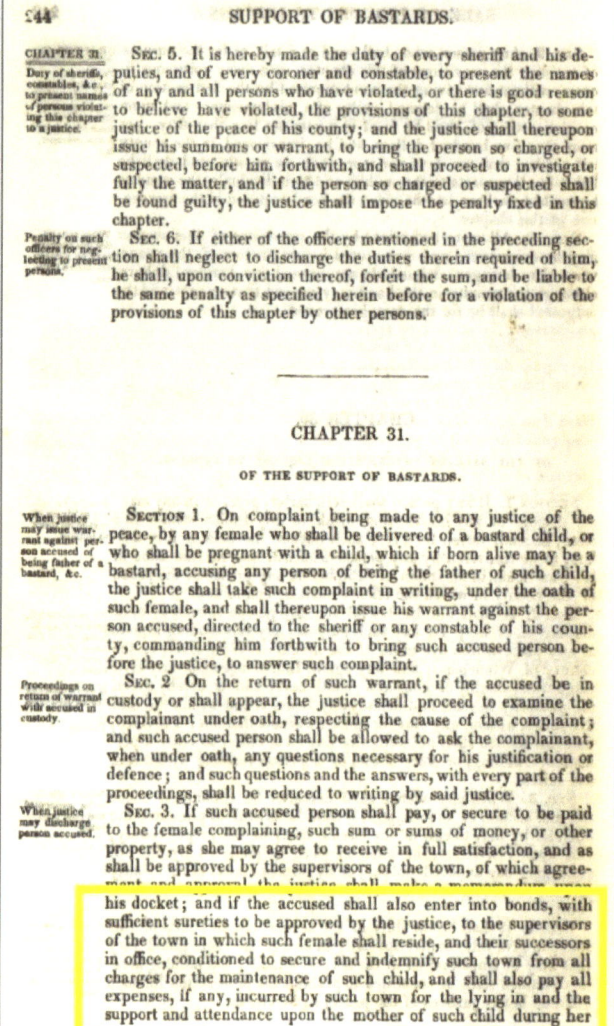

Figure 67: *Acts*, ch.31 (Wis., 1848)

18 Wisconsin Statutes § 767.805(4)(d)(1) *(Voluntary acknowledgement of paternity; Acts 1997 ch.191 as 767.62, renumbered in Acts 2005 ch.443)*
An order establishing the amount of the father's obligation to pay or contribute to the **reasonable expenses of the mother's pregnancy and the child's birth**. The amount established may not exceed one-half of the total actual and reasonable pregnancy and birth expenses. The order also shall specify the court's findings as to whether the father's income is at or below the poverty line established under 42 USC 9902 (2), and shall specify whether periodic payments are due on the obligation, based on the father's ability to pay or contribute to those expenses.

18 Wisconsin Statutes § 769.201(1m) *(Bases for jurisdiction over nonresident; Acts 1993 ch.326)*
In a proceeding to establish or enforce a support order or to determine parentage of a child, a tribunal of this state may exercise personal jurisdiction over a nonresident individual, or the individual's guardian or conservator, if any of the following applies:... (d) The individual resided in this state and provided **prenatal expenses** or support for the child.

Wyoming

Since Wyoming was briefly part of the Territory of Dakota, the 1862 bastardy legislation technically qualifies as the earliest. However, the resulting statute did not carry over to the Territory of Wyoming, nor was there any mention of prenatal requirement in any child support legislation for over a century. Thus, as its own entity, Wyoming gained requirements in 1929.

Wyoming's prenatal child support requirements had several amendments since the initial *Uniform Legitimacy Act* in 1929, taking on modern complexities of state-level child support systems. The core aspects of the requirements still exist in the modern implementation, just encapsulated within the newer text.

[Wyoming Statutes § 20-2-307(b)(vi)](#) (*Child support; SL 1929 ch. 45 § 1, HB107; amended several times, renumbered in [Laws 2000 ch. 34](#)*)
A court may deviate from the presumptive child support established by W.S. 20-2-304 upon a specific finding that the application of the presumptive child support would be unjust or inappropriate in that particular case. In any case where the court has deviated from the presumptive child support, the reasons therefor shall be specifically set forth fully in the order or decree. In determining whether to deviate from the presumptive child support established by W.S. 20-2-304, the court shall consider the following factors:

...

(vi) Any **expenses reasonably related to the mother's pregnancy and confinement** for that child, if the parents were never married or if the parents were divorced prior to the birth of the child;

Figure 68: *Session Laws*, ch.45 (Wyo., 1929)

[Wyoming Statutes § 20-2-401(f)](#) (*Medical support; SL 1929 ch. 45 § 21, HB107; amended several times, renumbered in [Laws 2000 ch. 34](#)*)
In any action to establish or modify a child support obligation and upon a sufficient showing by the department of family services that birth costs were paid by medical assistance within the preceding five (5) years, **the court shall also order that the father pay birth costs to the department** in the manner set forth in W.S. 14-2-1001 through 14-2-1008. Failure of the department to make a sufficient showing under this subsection shall not preclude the department from subsequently seeking recovery in any other manner authorized by law.

Figure 69: *Session Laws*, ch.45 (Wyo., 1929)

District of Columbia

District of Columbia Official Code, § 16-2349(a)
(Judgment; Pub. L. 88-241, 1963)
Prenatal and Confinement Expenses; Maintenance. — When the defendant in a proceeding pursuant to this subchapter, in open court acknowledges the paternity of a child born out of wedlock, or when, **at the trial the finding of the court or jury is against the defendant, the court, in rendering judgment, may enter an order for the payment of the prenatal medical care and costs of the mother's confinement and expenses of childbirth in such amount or amounts as it deems reasonable, commensurate with defendant's ability to pay**. The court may also order payments for the maintenance and education of the child, commensurate with defendant's ability to pay, to be made at such periods or intervals as the court directs. The court may order payments to be made by the defendant at a precinct of the Metropolitan Police Department of the District of Columbia. Payments shall continue until the child reaches the age of 16 years, unless, prior thereto, the child is legally adopted.

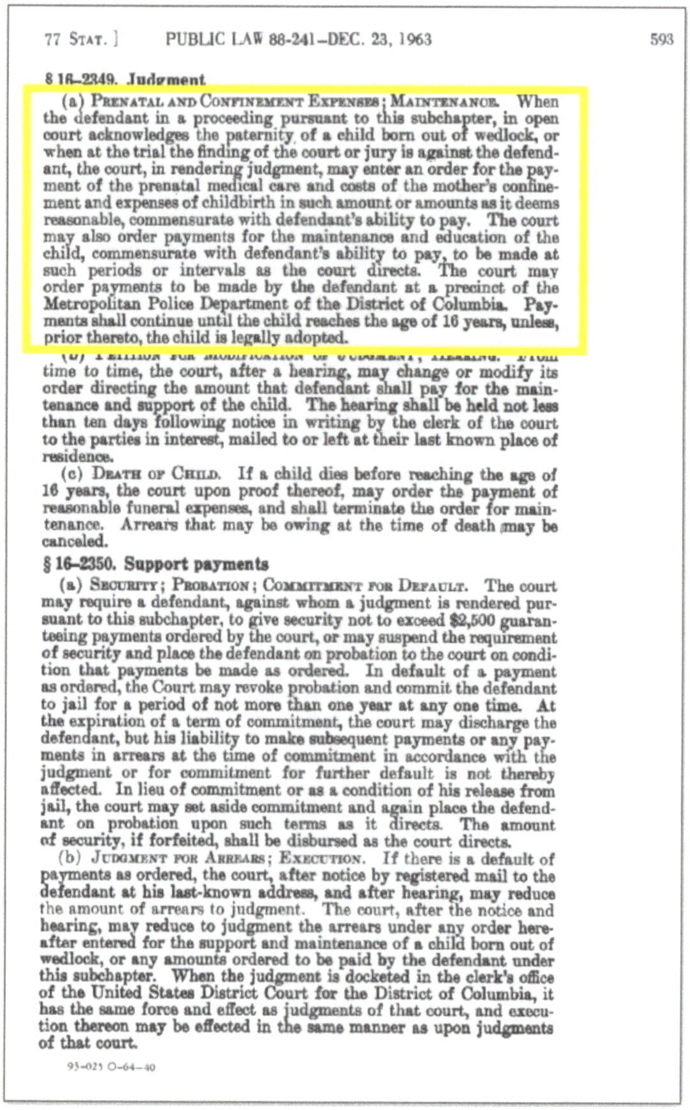

District of Columbia Official Code § 46-302.01(a) *(Bases for Jurisdiction over Nonresident; Law 11-81 § 201, 1996 as § 30-342.1)*
In a proceeding to establish or enforce a support order or to determine parentage, the Family Division may exercise personal jurisdiction over a nonresident individual or the individual's guardian or conservator, if:... (4) The individual resided in the District and **provided prenatal expenses** or support for the child;

District of Columbia Official Code § 46-303.016(d) *(Special Rules of Evidence and Procedure; Law 11-81 § 315, 1996 as § 30-343.15)*
Copies of bills for testing for parentage, and for **prenatal and postnatal health care of the mother and child**, furnished to the adverse party at least 10 days before trial, are admissible in evidence to prove the amount of the charges billed and that the charges were reasonable, necessary, and customary.

Figure 70: *US Code Pub.L. 88-241 (1963)*

American Samoa

American Samoa Code Annotated § 45.1505(c)(4)
(Paternity Proceedings; 1980 PL 16-71 § 1)
The order may direct the father to **pay necessary expenses incurred by or for the mother in connection with her confinement and any expenses in connection with her pregnancy** as the Court may find proper.

45.1505 Orders.

Chapter 15 - Paternity Proceedings

(a) If the Court finds the respondent is not the father of the child, it dismisses the petition.

(b) If the Court finds the respondent is the father of the child, it makes an order declaring paternity.

(c) (1) In a proceeding in which the Court has made an order declaring paternity, the Court may order the father to pay weekly or at other fixed periods, a fair and reasonable sum for the support and education of the child until the child is 18 years of age, or until the child is 21 years of age in the discretion of the Court, unless the support order is terminated sooner because the child becomes self-supporting or is legally emancipated. The Court takes into consideration other persons legally entitled to support by the father.

(2) The Court may order a father to pay for the support of his child after the child is 21 years of age if the child is unable to care for himself by reason of mental or physical handicap or other reason justifiable in the opinion of the court.

(3) The order declaring paternity may also direct the father to pay for support of the child prior to the order.

(4) The order may direct the father to pay necessary expenses incurred by or for the mother in connection with her confinement and any expenses in connection with her pregnancy as the Court may find proper.

(5) The Court may order payments made to the mother or to some other person or agency who shall administer them under the supervision of the Court.

(d) The Court may require the father to enter a bond as surety that the order of support will be carried out.

(e) The Court may modify an order of support upon proof of change in relevant circumstances.

(f) The Court may assess the costs of the action as part of its order.

Figure 71: *American Samoa Code Annotated*, § 45.1505

Guam

The *Guam Legislature* established the *Child Support Enforcement Office* in 1981 during the sixteenth regular legislative session.[32] Prenatal child support came in two separate bills during the twenty-fourth legislative session, in 1997 and 1998.

5 Guam Code Annotated § 34105(a)(7) *(Basis for Jurisdiction over Nonresident; PL 24-116 § 7, 1997; SB355)*
To recover necessary **expenses incurred by or for the mother in connection with the birth of her child,** for the funeral expenses if the child has died, for **expenses incurred in connection with pregnancy of the mother**, except as limited by (b) of this Section;

amounts as may be due and owing under an existing court order, whether owed to the Department or to the custodial parent or other person having custody of the minor child;

(2) For a continuing order of support for the benefit of such children;

(3) To establish paternity;

(4) To move to modify existing orders up or down as the circumstances and equity demand;

(5) To obtain orders of wage assignment;

(6) To recover amounts for which a parent is legally liable to Guam as a result of public assistance having been granted due to the separation or desertion of the parent from his or her child or children;

(7) To recover necessary expenses incurred by or for the mother in connection wit the birth of her child, for the funeral expenses if the child has died, for expenses incurred in connection with pregnancy of the mother, except as limited by (b) of this Section, and

(8) To recover reimbursement of the cost of support for the child before the commencement of the action, determined by using the appropriate Child Support Guidelines currently in effect, except as limited by (b) of this section.

(b) If an action is commenced after the lapse of more than six (6) years from the birth of the child, an amount shall not be awarded for expenses or support under (a)(7)-(8) of this Section that accrued before

15

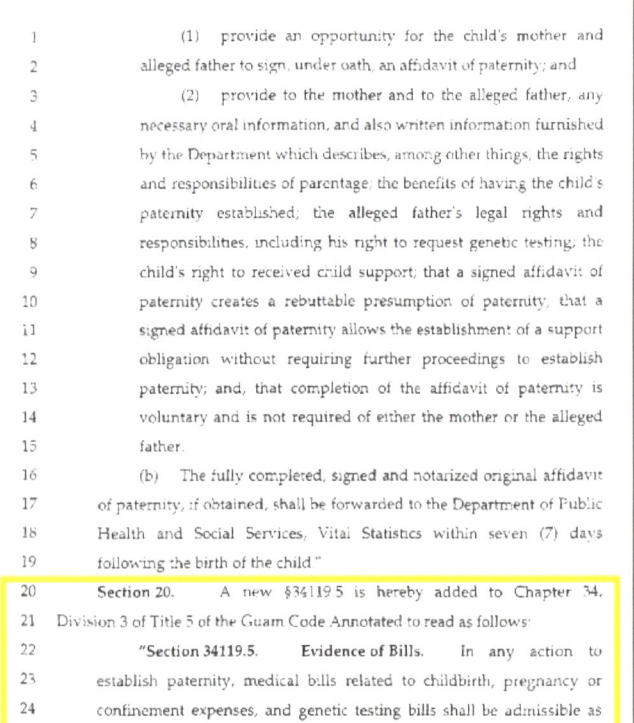

Figure 72: Guam *Public Laws 24-116*, 1997

(1) provide an opportunity for the child's mother and alleged father to sign, under oath, an affidavit of paternity; and

(2) provide to the mother and to the alleged father, any necessary oral information, and also written information furnished by the Department which describes, among other things, the rights and responsibilities of parentage, the benefits of having the child's paternity established; the alleged father's legal rights and responsibilities, including his right to request genetic testing; the child's right to receive child support; that a signed affidavit of paternity creates a rebuttable presumption of paternity; that a signed affidavit of paternity allows the establishment of a support obligation without requiring further proceedings to establish paternity; and, that completion of the affidavit of paternity is voluntary and is not required of either the mother or the alleged father.

(b) The fully completed, signed and notarized original affidavit of paternity, if obtained, shall be forwarded to the Department of Public Health and Social Services, Vital Statistics within seven (7) days following the birth of the child."

Section 20. A new §34119.5 is hereby added to Chapter 34, Division 3 of Title 5 of the Guam Code Annotated to read as follows:

"Section 34119.5. Evidence of Bills. In any action to establish paternity, medical bills related to childbirth, pregnancy or confinement expenses, and genetic testing bills shall be admissible as evidence without foundation testimony, and shall constitute prima facie

20

Figure 73: Guam *Public Laws 24-129*, 1997

5 Guam Code Annotated § 34119.5 *(Evidence of Bills; PL 24-129 § 20, 1997; Bill 460)*
In any action to establish paternity, **medical bills related to childbirth, pregnancy or confinement expenses**, and genetic testing bills shall be admissible as evidence without foundation testimony, and shall constitute prima facie evidence of the amounts incurred.

Northern Mariana Islands

8 Commonwealth Code §1715(c) *(Uniform Parentage Act, Judgment or Order; 1984 PL No. 4-38 §15, HB163)*
The judgment or order may contain any other provision directed against the appropriate party to the proceeding, concerning the duty of support, the custody and guardianship of the child, visitation privileges with the child, the furnishing of bond or other security for the payment of the judgment, or any other matter in the best interest of the child. The judgment or order may direct the father to **pay the reasonable expenses of the mother's pregnancy and confinement.**

PUBLIC LAW NO. 4-38
H.B. No, 163, H.D.1

(c) The judgment or order may contain any other provision directed against the appropriate party to the proceeding, concerning the duty of support, the custody and guardianship of the child, visitation privileges with the child, the furnishing of bond or other security for the payment of the judgment, or any other matter in the best interest of the child. The judgment or order may direct the father to pay the reasonable expenses of the mother's pregnancy and confinement.

(d) Support judgments or orders ordinarily shall be for periodic payments which may vary in amount. In the best interest of the child, a lump sum payment or the purchase of an annuity may be ordered in lieu of periodic payments of support. The court may limit the parent's liability for past support of the child to the proportion of the expenses already incurred that the court deems just.

(e) In determining the amount to be paid by a parent for support of the child and the period during which the duty of support is Owed, a court enforcing the obligation of support shall consider all relevant facts, including

(1) the needs of the child;

(2) the standard of living and circumstances of the parents;

(3) the relative financial means of the parents;

(4) the earning ability of the parents;

Page 13

Figure 74: *Public Laws*, No. 4-38 (NMI, 1984)

Puerto Rico

Official laws of Puerto Rico are written in Spanish, then translated to English for secondary publication. Thus, if there are any ambiguities to the English text, the territory can reference the Spanish originals. I have chosen to include the original Spanish versions as the images and the English translations as the body text.

8 Laws of Puerto Rico Annotated § 510(d) *(Special Child Support Act, Expedited administrative procedure;* Ley 169-1997, PC1278*)*

In any procedure under this section, **pregnancy** or genetic test expense related receipts shall be admissible as evidence without requiring witness corroboration by third parties and shall constitute prima facie evidence of the expenses incurred for these services or tests in behalf of the minor or minors.

En cualquier procedimiento iniciado a tenor con este artículo, cualquier recibo, informe médico o comprobante por embarazo, parto o pruebas genéticas será admisible en evidencia, sin requerir testimonio corroborativo de terceras partes, y constituirá evidencia prima facie de su contenido y de los gastos incurridos por estos servicios o por los exámenes efectuados en favor del menor o los menores.

La prueba genética será admisible sin necesidad de prueba corroborativa u otra prueba de autenticidad o certeza, a menos que se radique objeción justificada por escrito ante el Examinador y se notifique a la parte contraria dentro del término de veinte (20) días a partir de la notificación del informe del resultado de la prueba, o antes de los diez (10) días de la fecha de la primera vista que se señale para esos efectos, pero bajo ninguna circunstancia después. En caso de que se radique una objeción a la prueba genética, sólo se ordenarán pruebas adicionales si la parte que objeta radica una petición justificada para pruebas adicionales y provee el pago por adelantado para cubrir el costo de las mismas. Si se presenta en tiempo una objeción, la admisibilidad del resultado será determinada por el Examinador en forma justa y razonable. El costo de las pruebas genéticas originales se recobrará a favor de la parte que prevalezca, pero los costos no podrán recobrarse de un individuo que reciba beneficios del Programa de Asistencia Temporal del Departamento o del Programa de Ayuda a Médico Indigentes (Medicaid).

d .

..."

Sección 13.-Se enmienda el Artículo 17 de la Ley Núm. 5 de 30 de diciembre de 1986, según enmendada, para que se lea como sigue:

"Artículo 17.-Orden de pensión alimenticia provisional.-

En adición a lo dispuesto en los Artículos 15, 16 y 18 (2) de esta Ley, el Examinador recomendará la fijación de una pensión alimenticia provisional cuando, a solicitud de cualesquiera de las partes o por alguna otra razón, se disponga la posposición de una vista, faltare alguna información o pruebas, se refiera el caso al juez o se transfiera el caso a otra sala o sección del Tribunal, o cuando las necesidades del alimentista sean tan urgentes que así se requiera, excepto en los casos en que la paternidad del alimentista esté en controversia. No obstante, aún en los casos en que la paternidad está en controversia de existir evidencia clara y convincente sobre paternidad que esté fundamentada en prueba genética de paternidad o cualquier otra evidencia

Figure 76: *Leyes*, No. 169 (PR, 1997)

menos que se radique una objeción por escrito ante el Administrador o Juez Administrativo y se le notifique a la parte contraria en un período no menor de veinte (20) días luego del recibo del informe sobre la prueba genética, pero nunca menor de diez (10) días de antelación a la fecha de la vista. Si se radica una objeción a la prueba genética, se deberá ordenar prueba adicional sólo si la parte objetante radica una solicitud de prueba adicional y provee pago por adelantado del costo de la prueba.

Así también, se presumirá controvertible la paternidad en aquellos casos en que el examen genético ordenado por el Administrador o el Juez Administrativo produzca una probabilidad de paternidad de noventa y cinco (95) a noventa y siete punto nueve (97.9) por ciento, pero el peso de probar que no es padre recaerá sobre el alegado padre. Se presumirá incontrovertible la paternidad en los casos en que el examen genético ordenado por el Administrador o el Juez Administrativo produzca una probabilidad de paternidad de noventa y ocho (98) por ciento en adelante.

A fin de que el Administrador o Juez Administrativo pueda emitir una decisión final en los casos donde exista controversia sobre la paternidad, deberá demostrarse en el récord los elementos prima facie demostrativos de la paternidad.

C .

...

D.En cualquier procedimiento bajo este Artículo, cualquier recibo por concepto de gastos de embarazo, parto o prueba genética será admisible en evidencia como evidencia sin requerir testimonio corroborativo de terceras partes y constituirá evidencia prima facie de las cantidades incurridas por estos servicios o por las pruebas en favor del menor o menores.

E.En cualquier procedimiento bajo este Artículo, si existe evidencia clara y convincente, basada en las pruebas genéticas y otra evidencia creíble, se emitirá una orden provisional requiriendo una pensión alimentaria de menores mientras se dicta una determinación de paternidad del Administrador, Juez Administrativo o el Tribunal.

Todas las órdenes emitidas a tenor con este Artículo deberán contener una disposición que requiera a todas las partes en el caso informar a la Administración sobre cualquier cambio en su dirección residencial, lugar de empleo o ambos, o cambios en la cubierta de seguro médico disponible,

Figure 75: *Leyes*, No. 169 (PR, 1997)

8 Laws of Puerto Rico Annotated § 512(2)(c) *(Special Child Support Act, Expedited legal procedure;* Ley 169-1997, PC1278*)*

Concerning any procedure initiated under this section, any **receipt, medical report or proof of pregnancy, delivery** or genetic test shall be admissible as evidence without requiring corroborative testimony of third parties and shall constitute prima facie evidence of its contents and of the expenses incurred for these services or for the tests conducted in favor of the minor or minors.

US Virgin Islands

As with a few remaining states and territories in the late 1990s, the US Virgin Islands explicitly enacted prenatal child support for Federal compliance requirements relating to *Title IV-D* "Child Support Enforcement Programs" (referenced on the next page), under the *Personal Responsibility and Work Opportunity Reconciliation Act* (1996)[33]. Yet, the US Virgin Islands went beyond the minimum and added requirements for postnatal care to cover hospital costs immediately following birth.

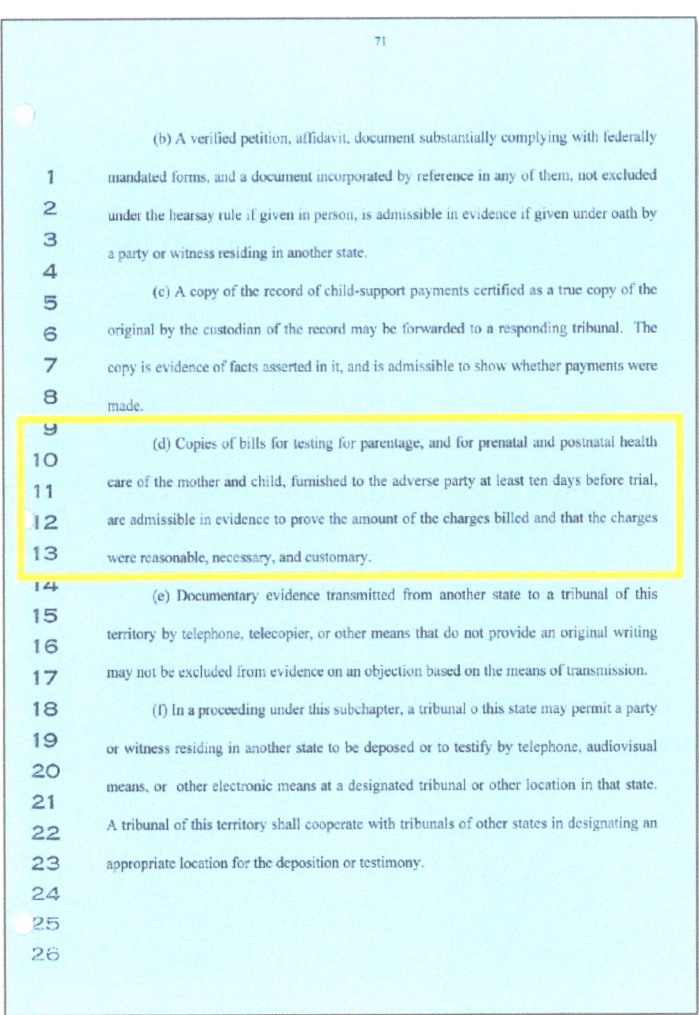

Figure 77: *Acts*, 6228 (VI, 1998)

[Virgin Islands Code Title 16, Chapter 13, Subchapter III § 396(d)](#) *(Bases for Jurisdiction over Nonresident; [Act 6228 1998 § 17, Bill 22-0176](#))*
the individual resided in this territory and **provided prenatal expenses** or support for the child;

[Virgin Islands Code Title 16, Chapter 13, Subchapter III § 420(d)](#) *(Special Rules of Evidence and Procedure; [Act 6228 1998 § 17, Bill 22-0176](#))*
Copies of bills for testing for parentage, and for **prenatal and postnatal health care of the mother and child**, furnished to the adverse party at least ten days before trial, are admissible in evidence to prove the amount of the charges billed and that the charges were reasonable, necessary, and customary.

Federal

At the Federal level, the *United States Code* has seen numerous child support additions and amendments throughout the twentieth century and into the twenty-first century. These have addressed topics relating to enforcement, domestic reciprocity, international reciprocity, and several other matters. For the most part, states and territories are semi-autonomous with how they enact their child support laws, only requiring specific aspects of Federal law to meet minimum uniform compliance under *US Code* sections like *Title IV-D* of the *Social Security Act*[34] — which is the only one to address prenatal child support.

42 United States Code §666(a)(5)(K) *(Personal Responsibility and Work Opportunity Reconciliation Act of 1996, Proof of Certain Support and Paternity Establishment Costs;* Pub. L. 104–193 §331*)*

Procedures under which **bills for pregnancy, childbirth**, and genetic testing are admissible as evidence without requiring third-party foundation testimony, and shall constitute prima facie evidence of amounts incurred for such services or for testing on behalf of the child.

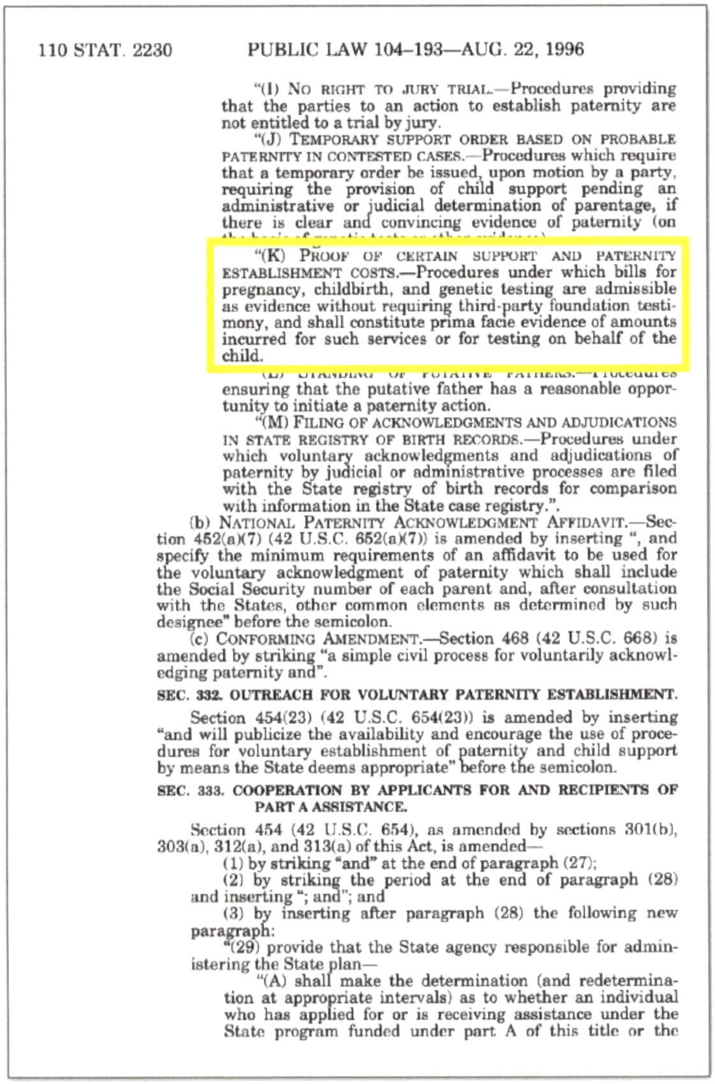

110 STAT. 2230 PUBLIC LAW 104–193—AUG. 22, 1996

"(I) NO RIGHT TO JURY TRIAL.—Procedures providing that the parties to an action to establish paternity are not entitled to a trial by jury.

"(J) TEMPORARY SUPPORT ORDER BASED ON PROBABLE PATERNITY IN CONTESTED CASES.—Procedures which require that a temporary order be issued, upon motion by a party, requiring the provision of child support pending an administrative or judicial determination of parentage, if there is clear and convincing evidence of paternity (on the basis of genetic tests or other evidence).

"(K) PROOF OF CERTAIN SUPPORT AND PATERNITY ESTABLISHMENT COSTS.—Procedures under which bills for pregnancy, childbirth, and genetic testing are admissible as evidence without requiring third-party foundation testimony, and shall constitute prima facie evidence of amounts incurred for such services or for testing on behalf of the child.

"(L) STANDING OF PUTATIVE FATHERS.—Procedures ensuring that the putative father has a reasonable opportunity to initiate a paternity action.

"(M) FILING OF ACKNOWLEDGMENTS AND ADJUDICATIONS IN STATE REGISTRY OF BIRTH RECORDS.—Procedures under which voluntary acknowledgments and adjudications of paternity by judicial or administrative processes are filed with the State registry of birth records for comparison with information in the State case registry.".

(b) NATIONAL PATERNITY ACKNOWLEDGMENT AFFIDAVIT.—Section 452(a)(7) (42 U.S.C. 652(a)(7)) is amended by inserting ", and specify the minimum requirements of an affidavit to be used for the voluntary acknowledgment of paternity which shall include the Social Security number of each parent and, after consultation with the States, other common elements as determined by such designee" before the semicolon.

(c) CONFORMING AMENDMENT.—Section 468 (42 U.S.C. 668) is amended by striking "a simple civil process for voluntarily acknowledging paternity and".

SEC. 332. OUTREACH FOR VOLUNTARY PATERNITY ESTABLISHMENT.

Section 454(23) (42 U.S.C. 654(23)) is amended by inserting "and will publicize the availability and encourage the use of procedures for voluntary establishment of paternity and child support by means the State deems appropriate" before the semicolon.

SEC. 333. COOPERATION BY APPLICANTS FOR AND RECIPIENTS OF PART A ASSISTANCE.

Section 454 (42 U.S.C. 654), as amended by sections 301(b), 303(a), 312(a), and 313(a) of this Act, is amended—

(1) by striking "and" at the end of paragraph (27);

(2) by striking the period at the end of paragraph (28) and inserting "; and"; and

(3) by inserting after paragraph (28) the following new paragraph:

"(29) provide that the State agency responsible for administering the State plan—

"(A) shall make the determination (and redetermination at appropriate intervals) as to whether an individual who has applied for or is receiving assistance under the State program funded under part A of this title or the

Figure 78: *US Code Pub.* L. 104-193 (US, 1996)

Endnotes

[1] *Hathi Trust Digital Library*. https://www.hathitrust.org

[2] *Google*, "Google Scholar." https://scholar.google.com

[3] *Library of Congress*. https://www.loc.gov

[4] *Patreon*, "Daniel Gump." https://www.patreon.com/danielgump

[5] *Living Infants Fairness and Equality (LIFE) Act.* House Bill 481. (Ga., 2019). http://www.legis.ga.gov/Legislation/20192020/187013.pdf

[6] *Official Code of Georgia Annotated.* (Ga., 2020) https://advance.lexis.com/container?config=00JAAzZDgzNzU2ZC05MDA0LTRmMDItYjkzMS0xOGY3MjE3OWNIODlKAFBvZENhdGFsb2cIFfJnJ2lC8XZi1AYM4Ne&crid=bcf88522-46e8-4962-a259-2bddbaf14e87&prid=475273c0-638f-4737-86cd-2db0ac21b734 (provides link to Lexis Nexis landing page)

[7] Green, Lewis C., et al. "Uniform Parentage Act" (1973). *Uniform Law Commission*. https://www.uniformlaws.org/HigherLogic/System/DownloadDocumentFile.ashx?DocumentFileKey=24e42c1a-59ac-b0b7-d35b-7900b6093dc8&forceDialog=0.

[8] *Uniform Law Commission*. https://www.uniformlaws.org/

[9] *United States Code*. https://uscode.house.gov

[10] Gump, Daniel. "A Discussion of Prenatal Child Support Laws" *Human Defense Initiative*. February 5, 2020. https://humandefense.com/a-discussion-of-prenatal-child-support-laws/

[11] *South Dakota Codified Laws* § 25-8-3. "Father and mother's liability for confinement expense" (SD, 1939) https://sdlegislature.gov/Statutes/Codified_Laws/DisplayStatute.aspx?Type=Statute&Statute=25-8-3

[12] *Nebraska Revised Statutes* § 43-1407 "Liability of father" (Neb., 1941) https://nebraskalegislature.gov/laws/statutes.php?statute=43-1407

[13] *South Dakota Code of 1939*. (SD, 1939) sdsdl-montage.auto-graphics.com/#/item-details/entities_3654?from=search-results

[14] *Session Laws 1923*, ch. 295 "Uniform Illegitimacy Act." (SD, 1923). sdsdl-montage.auto-graphics.com/#/item-details/entities_5985?from=search-results

[15] Kentucky Children's Code Commission. *Report of The Kentucky Children's Code Commission*. "Illegitimacy" p.71 (Ky., 1923) https://babel.hathitrust.org/cgi/pt?id=uiug.30112039962946&view=1up&seq=79

[16] *Personal Responsibility and Work Opportunity Reconciliation Act*, Pub. L. 104-193. "Proof of Certain Support and Paternity Establishment Costs" (US, 1996) https://www.govinfo.gov/content/pkg/PLAW-104publ193/pdf/PLAW-104publ193.pdf

[17] Tom Kyne, Jr., v. Tom Kyne (38 Cal. App. 2d 122, 1940) https://law.justia.com/cases/california/court-of-appeal/2d/38/122.html

[18] *LIFE Act*. Ibid.

[19] Cobb, Thomas R.R. *1851 Cobb's Digest (Vol. 1)*. "Bastardy," pp.148-149. (1851) https://digitalcommons.law.uga.edu/ga_code/4/

[20] *Uniform Support of Dependents Law* for the *Public Assistance Code*, §4(b) p.2539. House Bill 869. "Jurisdiction and powers of court." (Ill., 1949)

[21] *Public Acts 79-474* § 10.1. "Jurisdiction and powers of court." (Ill., 1975)

[22] *Iowa Code of 2015* (Iowa, 2015) https://www.legis.iowa.gov/docs/shelves/code/ocr/2015%20Iowa%20Code.pdf

[23] *Iowa Code of 1924* (Iowa, 1924) https://www.legis.iowa.gov/docs/shelves/code/ocr/1924%20Iowa%20Code.pdf

[24] Kentucky Children's Code Commission. Ibid.

[25] Daggett, Harriet Spiller. *A Compilation of Louisiana Statutes Affecting Child Welfare and The Report of the Louisiana Children's Code Committee*. p.343. 1933. Louisiana State University. https://babel.hathitrust.org/cgi/pt?id=uva.x030789986&view=1up&seq=371

[26] *William Holmes v. Walter Mitchell et al.* Chancery court, jurisdiction unknown (Md., 1850) PDF pages: aomol.msa.maryland.gov/000001/000200/pdf/am200d--162.pdf, aomol.msa.maryland.gov/000001/000200/pdf/am200d--163.pdf, aomol.msa.maryland.gov/000001/000200/pdf/am200d--164.pdf, aomol.msa.maryland.gov/000001/000200/pdf/am200d--165.pdf, aomol.msa.maryland.gov/000001/000200/pdf/am200d--166.pdf, aomol.msa.maryland.gov/000001/000200/pdf/am200d--167.pdf

[27] *House Bill 1596*. "§ 1.205 Life begins at conception." (Mo., 1986) http://cdm16795.contentdm.oclc.org/cdm/compoundobject/collection/molaws/id/64058/rec/5

[28] *Missouri Revised Statutes,* § 1.205 "Life begins at conception." (Mo., 1986) https://revisor.mo.gov/main/OneSection.aspx?section=1.205&bid=65&hl=

[29] *Hanisky v. Kennedy* (56 N.W. 208, 1893). https://case-law.vlex.com/vid/56-n-w-208-619913286

[30] *Smith's Laws* (1 Sm.L.27, Ch.CXXII pp.27-29,1810) http://www.palrb.us/smithlaws/browse/smlspselectvolume.php

[31] *Family Code*, § 15.02 "Involuntary termination of parental rights." (Texas, 1974) http://www.sll.texas.gov/assets/pdf/historical-statutes/1974-1/1974-1-wests-texas-statutes-and-codes.pdf

[32] *Public Laws 16th Guam Legislature*, ch.10. Bill No. 308. (Guam, May 1981) http://guamlegislature.com/Public_Laws_16th/PL%2016-10.pdf

[33] *Personal Responsibility and Work Opportunity Reconciliation Act*. Ibid.

[34] The United States Department of Justice. "Child Support Enforcement" Accessed July 11, 2020. https://www.justice.gov/criminal-ceos/child-support-enforcement

www.ingramcontent.com/pod-product-compliance
Lightning Source LLC
Chambersburg PA
CBHW051202220526
45473CB00003B/871